Re-writing St Kilda

New Views on Old Ideas

*The Proceedings of a three-day Conference
held in the Isle of Benbecula,
11–14 August 2010*

Edited by Bob Chambers

The Islands Book Trust

Published in 2011
by The Islands Book Trust

www.theislandsbooktrust.com

ISBN: 978-1-907443-23-7

© of the individual chapters remains with the named authors

British Library Cataloguing in Publication Data. A CIP record
for this book can be obtained from the British Library.

Typeset by Erica Schwarz
Printed and bound by Martins the Printers, Berwick upon Tweed
Cover design by Jim Hutcheson

The Islands Book Trust
Ravenspoint Centre
Kershader
South Lochs
Isle of Lewis
HS2 9QA
Tel: 01851 880737

Contents

St Kilda 2010 Conference Review
Donald E. Meek 1

Hiort in Pre-1930 Writings – An Overview
Bill Lawson 6

Voices from St Kilda in the School of Scottish Studies
    Archives
Cathlin Macaulay 35

Naturalists and the 'St Kilda Library'
John A. Love 64

The Natural History of St Kilda
Richard Luxmoore 76

The Historiography of the Archaeology of St Kilda
Susan Bain 78

'Eileanaich Cian a' Chuain' / 'The Remote Islanders of the
    Sea'? Towards a Re-examination of the Role of Church and
    Faith in St Kilda
Donald E. Meek 90

The Memoirs of the Rev. Donald John Gillies
John Randall 149

A History of Photography in St Kilda
Martin Padget 158

Some Additional Notes on the Lantern Slides of St Kilda
Mark Butterworth 180

Recent Visitors to St Kilda: Attitudes, Perceptions and
    Responses
Jeff Stone 190

A St Kilda Diary
David Boddington 202

The Literature of the Great Blasket (An Blascaod Mor):
    An Extraordinary Output
Mícheál de Mórdha 206

Faroese Writing
Bergljót av Skarði 213

Islands Book Trust Commemorations to Mark the 80th
    Anniversary of the Evacuation of St Kilda 235

St Kilda 2010 Conference Review

Donald E. Meek

Conferences are usually like the proverbial curate's egg – good in parts. The conference commemorating the 80th Anniversary of the evacuation of St Kilda, and held at Lionacleit, Benbecula, was an outstanding exception to this general rule. Organised superbly by the Islands Book Trust, it was excellent throughout, with a wealth of engagement and illumination, relevant discussion, agreement and (courteous) disagreement – and an unforgettable trip to St Kilda for 22 participants on Saturday 14th August. The presence of close relatives of some of the St Kildan population added a special dimension. Neil Ferguson, grandson and namesake of the celebrated postmaster of St Kilda; Mrs Nancy MacDonald, widow of Lachie MacDonald; John MacDonald, son of Calum MacDonald; and Finlay Ross, a descendant of the MacKinnons at No 1, were a constant reminder of the all-important human dimension of these islands, and of the poignancy of evacuation and out-migration from Hirta. The 'St Kildans' were able to provide their own impressions of the island and its people in the course of the conference.

The aims of the conference – to examine the various '(mis) conceptions' which had arisen about the St Kilda archipelago and its people – were sketched out by the Chairman, John Randall, in his opening remarks on Wednesday 11th August. The heart of the enquiry focused on the 'historiography' of St Kilda, which, with over 700 books in print, must be regarded as one of the greatest 'island growth industries' of all time. What have been the biases, the assumptions, the unwarranted conclusions, which have shaped writers' (and also our own) perspectives? How different was the 'St Kilda experience' from that of the rest of the Hebrides? How does it compare with that of other islands, such as the now (similarly) depopulated Blasket Islands, off the south-west corner of Ireland?

The conference opened in fine style with a paper from the master-genealogist of the Western Isles, Bill Lawson, who raised fascinating questions about the perspectives of 'authoritative' accounts by visitors such as Martin Martin, and also about 'early' St Kildan tales, including the possibility that the natural store of island memory had absorbed and re-rooted stories which may have been imported from Skye when the population of Hirta had to be replenished with Sgitheanaich and Hearaich, following its near elimination by smallpox in the early eighteenth century. Story-telling by twentieth-century St Kildans, who had been recorded by the School of Scottish Studies in the 1950s and 1960s, was the theme of Cathlin Macaulay's presentation on Wednesday evening. Hearing St Kildans like Lachie MacDonald telling Gaelic stories, and recounting island practices in Gaelic and English, was deeply moving, as it provided indisputable evidence of the skills of island story-tellers, often thought to have been eliminated by the 'gloomy' post-1800 religion of the St Kildans. Those in the audience with an ear for Gaelic dialects could still hear cadences of Skye and Harris Gaelic in the story-tellers' voices. After the recordings, Nancy MacDonald was presented with a certificate making her an Honorary Member of the Islands Book Trust.

Thursday's programme began with an overview of the birdlife and ecology of St Kilda by Dr Richard Luxmoore. Dr Luxmoore's fascinating presentation demonstrated the immense significance of St Kilda to North Atlantic birdlife, both as a breeding area and as a sustainer of life, which, while having much in common with other islands, nevertheless accommodated distinctive species or sub-species, including the St Kilda fieldmouse. This was followed by a broad sweep through the pre-history and archaeology of St Kilda, by Susan Bain. With excellent use of slides, she showed the main areas of enquiry of interest to present-day archaelogists, and also demonstrated the fundamental concerns of archaeology as a discipline. Through painstaking excavation, it was possible to identify artefacts and structures which linked St Kilda to the conventions of other islands in the Hebrides, while there were, indeed, points of divergence. The theme of Hebridean similarities was further pursued in the afternoon by Donald Meek in his re-evaluation of the impact of religion, and especially post-1820 evangelical faith, on the St Kildans. Conventionally regarded as dark and repressive, it was not resented by such St Kildans as had written about it from their own perspective (most notably the Rev. Donald John Gillies and Calum MacDonald). In most respects, it was comparable with the form of the evangelical faith in the wider Outer Hebrides. Far from weakening St Kildan society, according to the speaker, it had strengthened it, as it interacted harmoniously, rather than destructively, with their work and culture, despite the regulations which pertained to issues such as Sabbath observance. The recently-published writings of both Donald John Gillies and Calum MacDonald were then examined and set in context by John Randall and John MacDonald, respectively. John Randall emphasised how different Gillies's perspectives on St Kilda's birdlife were from those of present-day scientists, while John MacDonald sketched a deeply moving portrait of his father, a St Kilda exile whose family had moved to Harris about 1924. Calum was living latterly in London, but he returned to his native island periodically. On Thursday evening, the focus moved to the portrayal of St Kilda in photographs and lantern slides, with a memorial presentation by Martin Padget on the work of several photographers from

3

Captain Thomas to Robert Atkinson, and by Mark Butterworth on the slides produced by George Washington Wilson and his St Kilda photographer, Norman MacLeod. Mark Butterworth's talk was presented by means of a magic lantern, which replicated the means and context of such 'showings' in the late nineteenth and early twentieth centuries.

Friday's presentations were concerned, broadly, with St Kilda in contemporary perspective. Jeff Stone provided a ground-breaking overview of post-evacuation 'visitors'' impressions of St Kilda, while Dr David Boddington, with great good humour, recounted several of his adventures while stationed in St Kilda in the 1950s. Wider comparative angles on St Kilda appeared in the afternoon, with a stimulating presentation on the Blasket Islands by Mícheál de Mórdha, who showed how the output of Irish literature about the Blaskets had been encouraged by a group of sympathetic scholars who visited the Great Blasket in the early twentieth century. St Kilda, by contrast, had received only ship-borne tourists, with no obvious concern for its Gaelic cultural heritage or for indigenous publications. Bergljot av Skardi, from the Faroe Islands, provided a fine overview of the development of modern Faroese literature. The presence of a Faroese speaker underlined comparisons between the Faroes and St Kilda, which had emerged in the course of the conference. The day was rounded off with a broad-brush discussion of such comparisons (and contrasts).

Hospitality and entertainment, provided by QinetiQ, Lionacleit School, and the Benebecula community, were memorable. So too was the trip to St Kilda on Saturday, which took place in fine weather. For the participants, it brought an outstanding conference to an extremely fitting conclusion. A highlight (among many such) was the launching of a St Kilda mailboat off Boreray by Neil Ferguson, grandson of the last postmaster of St Kilda. The conference was supported by the National Trust for Scotland.

BOOKS PUBLISHED BY THE ISLANDS BOOK TRUST IN CONJUNCTION WITH THE CONFERENCE

'Destination St Kilda – From Oban to Skye and the Outer Hebrides' edited by Mark Butterworth, price £19.99, plus P and P

'From Cleits to Castles' by Calum MacDonald, price £9.99, plus P and P

'St Kilda Diary – A Record of the Early Re-occupation of St Kilda' by Dr David Boddington, price £9.99, plus P and P

'Steamships to St Kilda – John McCallum, Martin Orme, and the Life and Death of an Island Community' by Donald Meek, price £7.50, plus P and P

All available via www.theislandsbooktrust.com or by phoning Margaret Macdonald on 01851 880737.

Hiort in Pre-1930 Writings – An Overview

Bill Lawson

There is no shortage of books and other writings on the subject of Hiort, but very few on the Hiortaich themselves. When we look at some of these writings, we can see how they categorise themselves into different types, largely dependent on when they were written, and what the literary fashions were at that time. We can begin with what I often think is the quintessential story of Hiort – how the MacLeods got the island. This version is from Lachlan MacLean's *Sketches of St Kilda* of 1838:

> *St Kilda was in the undisturbed possession of the solan goose and the other varied species of sea-fowl, which still lay claim to it, till the ninth century. About this time, as tradition says, the people of Harries and Uist, two rival clans, began to view it with a selfish eye, and disputes arose which of them should lord it. The question was soon put at rest by an expedient worthy of the times. It was mutually agreed upon that two currachs, one from Uist and one from Harries, should start at the same time, and that the boat that first made out to the island should declared for. Off set the two currachs, buffeting the astonished main with their yielding oars – each man was silent – each face lowered defiance – each heart, we may conceive, was the sport of fear and hope by alternations, on nearing the new empire.*

Towards evening, on approaching the goal, the Uist boat was a few strokes ahead and ready to seize the prize; which, when Colla 'Cloud or Macleod, master of the Harries Crew, saw, he seized his scian-dhu' and, with one determined stroke, cut off his left hand from the wrist, flung it ashore, and was unanimously declared rightful possessor, and Lord of St Kilda, as to this day.

Like so many of the stories about the island, it has drama, it has rivalry, it has pathos – and unfortunately it is quite untrue! Quite apart from the archaeological record, of which we are going to hear more, there is a charter by John of Isla to his son Reginald in 1346, '*de insula de Egge, de insula de Rume, de insula de Huwyste cum castro de Uynvawle, de insula de Barre et de insula de Hert*' – Eigg, Rum, Uist with the castle of Benbecula, Barra and Hirt. There is also a note in a *Manuscript History of the MacDonalds*, published in the *Transactions of the Iona Club*, that Godfrey MacDonald, son of John, Lord of the Isles '*gave Boysdale to MacNeill of Barra and gifted Hirta or St Kilda to the Laird of Harris*'. But however it came about, it is clear that by the 1500s, after the collapse of the Lordship of the Isles, Hiort was a part of the lands of MacLeod of Harris and Dunvegan.

The first detailed reference to the Hiortaich themselves is probably by Dean Monro in 1549. His description – '*simple creatures, scant learnit in any religion*' – is too well known to be worth quoting at further length here, and in any case there is reason to doubt whether his description was at first-hand.

W F Skene in his *Celtic Scotland* quotes a document, which from intrinsic evidence he dates from between 1577 and 1595 – '*Thair cummis na men furth from this Ile to oisting or weiris, because thay are but a poor barbarous people unexpert that dwellis in it, useand na kind of wappinis, but their daylie exercitation is maist in delving and labouring the ground, taking of foulis and gaddering their eggis, quhairon thay leif for the maist part of thair fude.'*

There is a tradition that one of the Spanish Armada galleons was wrecked on Mina Stac, by the catching of her mast on the roof of a natural arch. '*Nothing has been found there, even though three expeditions have made brief searches. However, the legend could almost equally be fitted by Geo Chaimbir, and this was confirmed when a cannon (about 1 metre long), partly jammed under a very large boulder was found by Eric Warburton in 1977. Also in this area are several lengths of large chain (with both ordinary and studded links) and pieces of wooden and metal wreckage lying in about 13 metres of water.'*

This is a grand example of why you should check even the most unlikely sources, for the quote comes from *St Kilda – a Submarine Guide* – by Gordon Ridley in 1983!

The main source for this early period is of course Martin Martin in his *A Late Voyage to St Kilda*, published in 1698. Martin has, quite fairly, been accused of playing up to his audience in stressing the oddity of the island and its people. It is also obvious that he went there in July, for I do not think that the famous quote – '*There is only this wanting to make them the happiest People in this habitable Globe – that they themselves do not know how happy they are*' – could have been penned in a February storm! Martin was with the Steward's party, going to Hiort to collect the rent – much of which was paid in kind, and consumed by the Steward and party during their visit, like a medieval monarch on progress. The allowance for each visitor of Martin's party was – '*beside a Barley Cake, eighteen of the eggs laid by the fowl called by them Lavy, and a greater number of the lesser eggs, as they differ in proportion. The eggs are found to be of an astringent and windy quality to Strangers, but it seems are not so to the Inhabitants, who are used to eat them from the nest. Our men upon their arrival eating greedily of them, became costive and feverish; they preserve their eggs commonly in their stone-pyramids, scattering the burnt Ashes of turf under and about them, to defend them from the air, dryness being their only preservative and Moisture their Corruption; they preserve them six, seven, or eight months, and then they become appetising and loosening, especially those that begin to turn.'*

It is usually quoted as one of attractions of St Kilda that there was more food available than you could possibly eat – but some of it was rather a specialist taste! Alexander Buchan, who

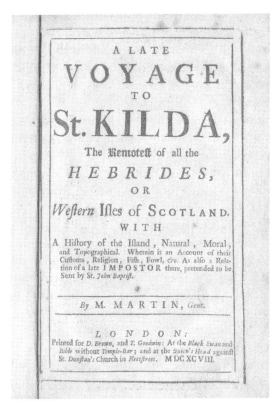

Title page of 'A Late Voyage to St Kilda' by Martin Martin

was on Hiort from 1704 to 1729 as schoolmaster, saw life there differently – '*They are in a manner prisoners, yea worse, all Things being considered; Prisoners in other places have the advantage of Visits from Friends and converse with them, which these poor people have not for the Greatest Part of the Year*' – but then he was from the mainland, and would have had friends elsewhere to converse with, which the Hiortaich themselves would not have had. He also notes that the crop of eggs and birds was much reduced from Martin's time, but whether from lack of birds or lack of gatherers is not clear. Buchan also noted that '*when the Steward and his followers come among them to demand his rents etc. viz. Down, Wool, Butter, Cheese, Cows, Sheep, Fowls, Oil etc, they look upon that visit as no great advantage to them and they very much grudge what he carries away with him and that they must be all the year toiling for others.*'

On the other hand, of course, the steward's visit was the only way in which the Hiortach could obtain necessities from outside their own rock-home and make contact with the outside world. It was during Buchan's stay on Hiort that a tragedy occurred which changed the very nature of the Hiortaich – to an extent which I feel is still not wholly appreciated by some writers. In 1727 a Hiortach visiting Harris had died of smallpox, and his gear was brought back to Hiort – and with it the infection. Three men and eight boys had been taken out to Stac an Armuinn, and left there to collect birds – and they were marooned there from August to May of the following year, when the Steward picked them up and took them home – to find that almost all the remaining Hiortaich had succumbed to smallpox. It is said that only four adults remained and 26 orphans – and it is not clear whether that included those who had been on the Stac. The Report of the SSPCK in 1731 suggests that '*Regard might be had to the people of Hirta, which Island, by the yearly transporting of people to it, will soon be populous again.*'

Rev. Kenneth MacAulay, who visited St Kilda in 1758 notes that '*the posterity of those who were the true natives of St. Kilda are distinguished by the sir-names of MacIlle Mhoire and MacIlle Riabhaich* (who) *value themselves not little upon their connection with the Captain of Clan Ranald.*' By the time of the first, unofficial, census of Hiort by Rev. John MacDonald of Ferintosh in 1820, the surnames on the island were still Morrison and MacDonald, with the addition of MacCrimmon, MacKinnon, MacQueen, Gillies and MacLeod – all of whom are thought to have come from MacLeod's estates in Skye – and Ferguson, the first of whom was from Berneray, Harris.

To my mind, this replacement of the native Hiortaich by newcomers from Skye explains many anomalies in the later history and traditions – not least the difference from Martin Martin's description – '*the men of St Kilda have generally but very thin beards, and these too do not appear until they arrive at the age of thirty, and in some not till after thirty-five; they have all but a few hairs upon the upper lip and point of the chin*' – which hardly agrees with the later pictures, for example, of the 'Parliament'! The Skye settlers brought their own traditions with them – among them I suspect the story of Fearchar and Dugan who burned the population in the Church – and I think that more care sometimes needs to be taken when considering the Hiortaich, whether it is the pre- or post-1727 Hiortaich who are being considered.

Post 1779

In 1779 Harris, including Hiort, was sold to Captain Alexander MacLeod of Berneray, former skipper of the East India trader *Mansfield*. Captain Alexander's aim was to develop Harris, and he developed the harbour at Rodel, the fishing stations around the Bays of Harris and even tried a fishery around St Kilda. '*In August 1785 he made a trial of the banks of St Kilda, which lies fifty-four miles west from the nearest lands of the Long Island. He sounded thirty miles round the former in every direction, and believes these banks extend still farther, being yet very little known. In June 1786 he sent out a stout boat, with expert fishermen, to make another trial of these banks. They met with great success, and he recommends a small bay on St. Kilda (the only one on that coast) as a place worthy of public notice, both on account of the fisheries and general navigation.'*

So said John Knox in his *A Tour through the Highlands of Scotland and the Hebride Isles in 1786*. He also tried to calculate the number of fish eaten by the gannets:

> *The solan goose is almost insatiably voracious; he flies with great force and velocity, toils all the day with very little intermission and digests his food in a very short time; he disdains to eat anything worse than a herring or mackerel, unless it be in a very hungry place, which he takes care to avoid or abandon. We shall take it for granted that there are 100,000 of that kind around the rocks of St Kilda; and this calculation is far too moderate, as no less than 20,000 of this kind are destroyed every year, including the young ones. We shall suppose, at the same time, that the solan geese sojourn in these seas for about seven months of the year; that each of them destroys five herrings in a day – a subsistence infinitely poor for so greedy a creature, unless it were more than half supported at the expence of other fishes. Here we have 100,000,000 of the finest fish in the world devoured annually by a single species of the St Kilda sea fowls.*

I can see his point, but am not quite sure about the maths!

Knox did not carry his notes to their logical conclusion, but this was done by John Sands in 1875:

> *It has been calculated that these birds devour 214,000,000 herring per annum, which is equivalent to 305,714 barrels –*

more than the total average of herrings barrelled at all the north-east stations – yet no attempt has been made to exterminate the solan geese and to secure the treasure which they consume!

John Lane Buchanan, writing in 1793, peppers his writing about the island with details which show that he was fully aware of his surroundings – '*the people of St Kilda from the nature of their food, emit a disagreeable odour. Fishes in general abound with much oil, and are often rancid upon the stomach, and affect the very sweat with a disagreeable smell, that offends the olfactory nerves of delicate constitutions.*'

Atkinson, on his visit in 1831 was more lucky – '*On our departure for St Kilda we were assured that we should imbibe a smell, from living among them, that would adhere to us for five or six weeks; fortunately the newly built parsonage house presented a comfortable and in-odorous habitation while we staid.*'

Having been greeted on my return from Sulaisgeir with the welcome – '*There's hot water and a change of clothing for you in the garage*' – I can appreciate their concern!

Many of the writers describe the methods of catching gannets, starting from Martin Martin, and each adds his own extra detail, but Buchanan's detailed account of gannet-catching does sound more like a fisherman's yarn:

The Solan Goose, after the hard toil of the day at fishing sleeps quite sound, in company with some hundreds and think themselves secure under the protection of a centinel. The fowler, with a white towel about his breast, calmly slides over the face of the rocks till he has a full view of the centinel; then he gently moves along on his hands and feet, creeping very silently to the spot where the centinel stands on guard. If he cries bir, bir, the sign of an alarm, he stands back; but if he cries grog grog, that of confidence,

> he advances without fear of giving an alarm, because the
> goose takes the fowler for one of the straggling geese coming
> in to the camp and suffers him to advance. Then the fowler
> very gently tickles one of his legs, which he lifts and places
> on the palm of his hand; he then as gently tickles the other,
> which in like manner is lifted and placed on the hand. He
> then no less artfully than insensibly moves the centinel near
> the first sleeping goose, which he pushes with his fingers; he
> immediately falls a-fighting him for his supposed insolence.
> This alarms the whole camp, and instead of flying off they
> all begin to fight through the whole company; while in the
> meantime the common enemy, unsuspected, begins in good
> earnest to twist their necks and never gives up till the whole
> are left dead on the spot.

Somehow I doubt whether it was quite so easy as that – but I do
like the picture of the fowler playing *gabh spog* with the gannet,
like a dog for a biscuit!

Buchanan was one of the first writers to show concern about
the economics of the island. We have already seen how the
Steward had to an extent obtained his rent by eating it on the spot,
but the last of the Clann Alasdair Ruaidh MacLeod stewards from
Pabaigh left for Carolina in 1773 and their successor, William
MacNeil, though perhaps connected to them through marriage,
viewed St Kilda purely as a source of income:

> Out of eighty acres of land they must pay fifty bolls of
> barley and potatoes yearly; and the Steward keeps his own
> dairy-maid on the islands to receive every drop of their
> milk from May to Michaelmas, to make butter and cheese
> for supplying his own table, and the remainder he sends
> to market. The high price of feathers and the immense
> quantities collected by these people increase the tacksman's
> income immensely.

Though Captain Alexander had an interest in developing Harris and Hiort, his successors had no interest other than collection of rental, and in 1804 St Kilda was sold to Lieut.-Col. Donald MacLeod of Auchnagoyle. From him it passed to his son John MacPherson MacLeod, who later sold it back to MacLeod of Dunvegan. In Donald MacLeod's time we begin to see the emergence of St Kilda as a tourist destination – with very different reactions:

Lord Brougham paid a visit in 1799 – and was not impressed!

At last came two boats, both manned by the savages. This alarmed us; we thought that our party must be lost or taken, and the arms-chest was instantly opened; but the boats approaching, we found the natives quite pacific. I always make a point of landing in full uniform. The view of this village is truly unique. Nothing in Captain Cook's voyages comes half so low. The natives are savage in due proportion; the air is infected by a stench almost unsupportable – a compound of rotten fish, filth of all kinds, and stinking sea-fowl. A total want of curiosity, a stupid gaze of wonder, an excessive eagerness for spirits and tobacco, a laziness only to be conquered by the hope of the above-mentioned cordials, and a beastly degree of filth, the natural consequence of this, render the St Kildian character truly savage.

One of his party, Robert Campbell of Shawfield, can hardly have been of the same opinions, for it was he whose dalliance with a St Kildan lass and his eventual abandonment of her gave rise to the song *Mo ghaol oigear a' chuil duinn*.

MacCulloch the geologist visited Hiort but his *Description* in 1819 seems to concentrate more on the inaccuracies of MacAulay, the stupidity of belief in *cratan nan gall* and a treatise on the history of the bagpipe and other Highland music. In his re-issue in 1824 he does give more detail of the village life – '*The air is full of feathered animals, the sea is covered with them, the houses are ornamented by them, the ground is speckled with them like a flowery meadow in May. The town is paved with feathers, the very dunghills are made of feathers, the ploughed land seems as if it had been sown with feathers, and the inhabitants look as if they had all been tarred and feathered, for their hair is full of feathers and their clothes are covered with feathers; everything smells of feathers and the smell pursued us all over the islands'* – but he still goes on about *cratan nan gall.*

This was the boat-cough – from Martin's time the Hiortaich claimed that they all caught a dose of the cold every time a visiting ship arrived. Hardly any of the writers believed them – yet who would have known better than the Hiortaich themselves, and of course modern medicine has shown that they were right.

1820–

In the early 1800s the most important visitors to the island were more concerned about the religious lot of the Hiortaich. What little education there had been in Buchan's time had virtually ceased, for although there was a titular school master and minister, he paid less and less attention to his island charge. According to one visitor in 1821 there was only one person on the island who could read or write. As always happens, everything then happened at once. A Gaelic school-teacher was appointed, who spent most of the next few years on the island, and by 1825 the teacher was able to report that there were 49 children in school.

Then in 1822 the island had the first of a series of visits from Rev. John MacDonald of Ferintosh, a leader in the evangelical wing of the Church, whose journals of his visits were published as addenda to the annual reports of the SSPCK. He was distressed to find no-one of a 'decidedly religious character' on the island, and preached thirteen sermons on his short visit. One cannot help feeling that so large an exposure, from an obviously educated man, of their overwhelming state of sin and its inevitable consequences, must have terrified the poor Hiortaich. Also, as Rev. Neil MacKenzie was to note on a later visit of MacDonald *'during his short stay on the island he preached several eloquent and powerful sermons, to which apparently they paid great attention; but I soon found that they were only charmed by his eloquence and energy, and had not knowledge enough to follow or understand his argument'.*

When MacDonald returned to the mainland he was instrumental in arranging for the building of a church and the employment of a resident minister, and on his third visit in 1827 the foundation stone of the church was laid. With MacDonald came Rev. Neil MacKenzie, who was to be the resident minister on the island for the next 16 years. Although MacKenzie was mainly concerned with the spiritual needs of his people, he was not unheeding of their practical needs as well, and provided what the community much needed – a leader. It was MacKenzie who led in the re-development of the land into crofts, in the building of the first set of houses on the Street, enclosure of the grave-yard etc. *Episode in the Life of the Rev. Neil MacKenzie at St Kilda from 1829 to 1843,* edited by his son Rev. John MacKenzie, is a gold-field of information about the island, its wildlife and its people, written by someone who was actually living there all the year round.

> *I got them persuaded after a little to build for themselves new houses on a more enlarged and better plan, but I could only get them to work when I wrought along with them. So long as I could be with them they would work quite eagerly, but whenever I had to leave, they soon got tired.*

> *Equal in their hopes and fears and habits, they in everything insisted upon an equality which had a deadening influence*

17

and effectually hindered any real progress. If anyone attempted to better himself he was set upon from all sides and persecuted by everyone. There must be no departure from what their fathers had done, unless, indeed, it were possible to do less. No one must be allowed to make himself much more comfortable than others.

Sir Thomas Dyke Acland had visited Hiort in 1812 and had been unfavourably impressed by the standard of housing in the old village, of which his sketches are almost the only visual record. He returned in 1834, to find little change, so, to encourage progress he left the sum of £20 to be used towards the building of new houses. With this inducement, MacKenzie persuaded the Hiortaich to move from their old run-rig system to a series of crofts, with each house along the street on its own croft, in a fan shape above the shore to the head dyke. With a little adjustment, this became the basis of the land-holding of the island, and is detailed in my own *Croft History of St Kilda*.

Acland has another claim to fame in St Kilda records. He called his yacht *The Lady of St Kilda* and after he sold her, she ended up in the coastal trade in Australia and was wrecked off Melbourne, giving her name to the beach which later became the site of St Kilda, Melbourne. St Kilda by this time found itself on the tourist route – if only the wealthier tourist. Lachlan MacLean's *Sketches of St Kilda* of 1838 are typically 'over the top' of their time.

If one would see Nature in her giant gambols, let him go to St Kilda. When the liquid foe, which knew no opposition since he left the North Pole – except perhaps an unfortunate ship, which he swallowed – sees St Kilda determined upon breaking his line – he retires a little, swelling as he retires in sullen wrath, and hurling with him stones, or rather fragments of rock, some of them 20, some 24 tons weight; then with these rude bullets in his grasp, hurling them against the island, he makes one desperate charge as if in hope to push the island from its seat! The purpose of the assailant is answered, however, in so far as that having mounted a rampart 1500 feet high, he gets over the island sheer, in white spray; dropping salt tears of disappointment upon the natives as he passes.

It was not only the British tourist who visited and wrote about the island. Frederic Mercey wrote his *Hirta – L'Isle des chasseurs* in 1842:

On n'a pas tort d'appeler cette ile escarpee le Teneriffe des iles Britanniques. Le Conachair, cette pointe que vous vovez la-haut, encapuchonnee de nuages, ne s'eleve pas, en effet, a moins de mille quatre cents pieds de hauteur au-dessus du niveau de l'Ocean. Voyez du cote de la mer, cette montagne est taillee si perpendiculairement, qu'un homme assis a son sommet pourrait pecher a la ligne dans l'Ocean, qui range sa basse, si toutefois sa ligne avait mille quatre cents pieds de longueur. Le hauteur de ce rocher est tellement extraordinaire, que, couche a plat ventre, du cote de precipice et regardant les flot au-dessous de vous, vous le voyer blancher de leur ecume le pied du rocher, et que votre oreille ne peut en entendre le bruit.

Another visitor who, in the absence of cameras, had the forethought to bring a tame artist with him was George C Atkinson. His *Expeditions to the Hebrides* is a most endearing book, and the illustrations are nothing if not dramatic.

We rowed to the bottom of the cliff formed by the hill of Conachar, to receive the fowl captured by a party who had been there since the morning; and here we had an opportunity of seeing in perfection their feats of climbing, on the loftiest precipice in Great Britain. On this occasion two young lads of 16 or 17 occupied our chief attention, as they had descended to within 50 or 60 feet of where our boat lay, and were noosing away at the Guillimottes on all sides with infinite success, chattering away with our boatmen in the intervals of their sport, and chucking bundles of dead birds from the nooks they had placed them in with more coolness than most men would look over a high bridge.

Another visitor during MacKenzie's time was James Wilson, whose *Voyage round the Coasts of Scotland and the Isles* is unusual for its time in its attention to small detail – '*In smaller enclosures here and there are what by courtesy may be called gardens, in which some cabbages and a few potatoes grow. The minister has tried both carrots and onions with some success. Turnips seem to thrive well for a time, but are speedily cut off by some kind of destructive insect, and peas and beans blossom, but produce no pods. The natives collect a considerable quantity of sea-fowl eggs in spring and the earlier part of the summer. They prefer them when sour, that is, as the minister expressed it, when about ten or twelve days old, and just as the incipient bird when boiled forms in the centre into a thickish flaky matter like milk.*'

Wilson also gives a vivid description of a show of cliff-dancing, as seen from the sea – '*Three or four men, from different parts of the cliff, threw themselves into the air, and darted some distance downwards, just as spiders drop from the top of a wall. They then swung and capered along the face of the precipice, bounding off at intervals by striking their feet against it and springing from side to side with as much fearless ease as if they were so many schoolboys exercising in a swing a few feet over a soft and balmy clover field. In this manner, shouting and dancing, they descended a long way towards us, though still suspended at a vast height in the air, for it would probably have taken all their cordage joined together to have reached the sea ... These men merely capered for our amusement, but caught no birds, for such was in fact the adamantine smoothness of the surface that not even a winged inhabitant of the air could have found rest for the sole of its foot.'*

But Wilson's main achievement was to take a census of the island, which had been forgotten in the national census of 1841 – '*We were surprised to find that although the census or enumeration of the inhabitants of the whole kingdom had recently been taken up, poor St Kilda had not even been regarded as belonging to the British dominions. No one there had ever heard of the census*' – nor, I am sure, were they in the least worried about it! Wilson notes 96 Hiortaich in 28 households, plus 9 in the manse. He also gives a great amount of detail about the birds and other wild-life there – how accurately I am not qualified to judge.

When MacKenzie left Hiort in 1843, there was great difficulty in finding a successor for him, and the Church of Scotland and the Free Church bickered for years over the ownership of the Church and provision of a minister. In the meantime, things had changed on the island. Rev. Neil MacKenzie had been instrumental in setting up a Kirk Session on the island, and this seems to have induced the Hiortaich to assert a greater role in deciding their own future. Little that happened in the outside world affected the Hiortaich, but in 1846 the Isle of Pabaigh was cleared of all its people, on the excuse of illicit distilling. Pabaigh had always been the base of the stewards of St Kilda, and there had been a small but steady movement of people, usually young men, from Hiort to Pabaigh and on to other parts of Harris, especially Scalpaigh. After 1846 this link was broken, so further increasing the isolation of the Hiortaich, and the difficulty of getting to the island.

In November 1852 eight families set off from Hiort to settle in Australia. There was no compulsion from their landlord to leave – in fact he met them in Liverpool and tried to persuade them to return. Malcolm MacQueen, one of the emigrants, quoted in his son Finlay's *Memoirs*, blamed the emigration on the dispute about ownership of the Church, but there was clearly more to it than that. MacQueen tells how this was intended to be an advance party, '*and the rest of the inhabitants would come away shortly*' but the emigrants were decimated by measles on ship and in quarantine.

Osgood MacKenzie in his *A Hundred Years in the Highlands* notes a visit to Hiort in May 1853 – '*Nearly all the male inhabitants of the island were assembled to meet us when we landed, as well might they welcome us, for they had not seen a creature but themselves for nine long months, and they were very anxious for news from Australia about their friends who had emigrated the previous autumn*' – but when the news of the disaster did arrive, naturally all thought of emigration was given up, at least for the meantime.

1850–

By the mid 1800s, we are into a period where the writings about St Kilda concentrate less on the marvels of the islands, though these of course could never be ignored, but more on the politics of the community – Hiortaich *v* landlord and Hiortaich *v* minister and schoolmaster, especially in the writings of Sands and Connell.

After a period of indecision John MacKay from Lochcarron was ordained in 1865, specifically for Hiort. MacKay was of a very different kind from MacKenzie, and took no share of leadership, or in the temporal life of his community. When John Sands first visited Hiort in 1875 he had nothing but praise for MacKay, but they fell out, and in the second edition of his journal *Out of the World or Life in St Kilda* MacKay is lampooned unmercifully – unfortunately few people have read the first edition! The subject on which they differed, and which exercised many writers in the subsequent period, was whether the Hiortaich would be better off trading their own produce directly with the mainland, which would doubtless produce better prices, or should they remain dependent on trade through the factor and MacLeod, which offered a safety-net. The Hiortaich, through the persuasion of MacKay, decided to remain with the factor – and Sands never forgave him! Sands also has another claim to fame – he was the sender of the first St Kilda mailboat – cast in the ocean with a favourable wind, in the hope of being cast ashore and picked up – which it, and a surprising number of its successors, indeed were!

Robert Connell visited Hiort as the correspondent of the *Glasgow Herald* in 1885, and he also was no friend of Rev. MacKay – '*There can be no manner of doubt that for much of the unhealthy moral atmosphere pervading the island at present the ecclesiastical authority in the person of Mr MacKay is mainly responsible. The weak-minded pope and prime-minister rolled in to one who rules the destinies of the island has reduced religion into a mere hypocritical formalism, finding no place in his creed for self-reliance or any of the manlier virtues. There is no use blinking the fact that during the twenty years the Reverend gentleman has held the island in his firm grip, no useful public work of any kind has been executed. At every point in the island one comes across evidences of the practical usefulness of a former minister, the Rev. Neil MacKenzie, under whose beneficent guidance the St Kildians appear to have put forth some energy to improve their condition. That however was in the good old days.*'

It has become customary to blame MacKay for all the ills of St Kilda, but there are some points to bear in mind. The first is that Hiort in his days sounds not greatly different from any other Free Church community in the Islands. Again the Free Church did not look on the economic welfare of their congregations as their prime responsibility – we may not agree with their stance, but we can hardly blame MacKay for following it. Also, as comes across to me strongly from the detailed research in Michael Robson's *St Kilda – Church, Visitors and Natives*, there seems to have developed a two-party state on Hiort, with the minister and his housekeeper on one side, and the Church elders on the other, with a continual power-struggle between them. Poor MacKay – after 20 years of isolation, no doubt his sermons were getting rather stale, but he seems to have been the subject of continual complaints. As an old man, and far too long isolated on the island, he was unable to deal with the rivalry that can so easily develop into a competition to see who can think of the more things which could be considered sinful!

If Connell's book has to be judged less than accurate, and heavily over-dramatised, we have to remember that he was a newspaper correspondent, and as we can still see today, an effective journalist may not be a reliable historian! But I can forgive him much, for a memorable phrase in his description of the church – '*Above your head are the bare rafters, with*

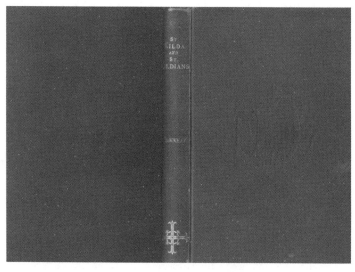

Connell's 'St Kilda and St Kildians'

numberless spiders performing profane somersaults while divine service is going on.'

John MacDiarmid of the Highland and Agricultural Society made a report in 1877 which includes a very full detail of the village and its people – here is a selection:

> *House 1   Donald McDonald, his wife, his mother, a servant and a boy his son 2 years old*
>
> *House 2   M McCrimmon – a widow & her son, who is unfit for work on account of a diseased leg*
>
> *House 3   Anne McDonald, a widow & her daughter. This woman's husband was drowned on the boat that left for the mainland about 13 or 14 years ago*
>
> *House 4   Malcolm McKinnon, wife and 1 son 9 years old. Had more of a family but all died when infants*

In the following year came George Seton's 350 page book, *St Kilda Past and Present*, the results of a four-hour visit to St Kilda. To be fair, his book is a very creditable recension of information from many earlier books – except Sands, whom he opposed tooth and nail, partly because of his own friendship with the MacLeod proprietors. Dissension between the elders and the minister continued after MacKay's departure and the appointment of Rev. Angus Fiddes, who did so much to assist the Hiortaich in their health, and in the erection of a proper pier, until he also decided to leave, in 1902. Thereafter no minister was appointed to Hiort, and probably none could be found willing to go there. In 1897 Hiort had a visit from Norman Heathcote and his sister Evelyn, cousins of the MacLeod proprietors. Heathcote's *St Kilda* is a perfectly adequate account of their visit, though it has little new in it, other than some excellent photographs. Evelyn, on the other hand, deserves to be remembered, if only for her description of the ascent of Stac Li:

Stack Li is only to be climbed on its southwest side, and against this landing place, if such it could be called, a heavy swell was breaking. We gazed despairing up at the 20ft of perpendicular rock, covered with slippery seaweed – not a nice place whereon to gain a footing at any time, even from a firm platform, but from a wildly-bouncing boat an apparent impossibility.

However, Finlay MacQueen is the best climber on the Island of St Kilda; and as soon as we could get near enough, he threw a rope over an iron peg fixed in the rock for that purpose; and this done, with another rope around his waist in case of accident, he sprang on to the face of the cliff and drew himself up to the first ledge, where he could make fast the rope and stand firmly himself ready to help as required. It was a wonderful performance! I did not feel encouraged to follow, but there was no time for consideration. The rope was soon around me, and up I went, like a bale of wool or a sack of potatoes!

She reached the very top of the stac, and put a stone on the cairn there, which was quite a feat, considering that the photographs show her wearing a long skirt and a straw boater. Even I have never been beyond the bothy on the shoulder!

1900–

There was however a succession of schoolmasters, several of whom left accounts of their stay. Of particular value are the diaries of Mrs MacLachlan, wife of the schoolmaster/missionary Peter MacLachlan, who was on the island from 1906–1909, from which the following are extracts.

Friday Jan 4th 1907

Fine day. Wind changed from NE to S. If the wind had continued the boats were going to Soay for sheep today but alas the wind has changed. However the trawlers may now come with the present wind. I am so much wearying for a boat to come though. I am longing for letters, potatoes, bacon, etc. Not to speak of newspapers, parcels.

Tuesday Oct 2nd 1906

As we were finishing our tea, we heard a great shouting and other confused noises. In a few moments the men were down, and in less time than it takes me to write they launched the boat, The women were screaming and wringing their hands, It seems that poor Norman Gillies, who had got away from school a little earlier than usual to go to Point of Coll to fish mullet, had fallen from the rocks into the sea. There is a fearful current there and although the only man there (Hugh Gillies) had flung him a rope, the current carried him out beyond it. Some of the bigger boys had run off home to give the news. Norman MacKinnon went to the place on foot, but only in time to see poor Norman sink. He was clinging to the fishing rod. He never made a sound. The boat was too late even to see him. We went up to the house with the men and women and stayed till nine o'clock and the sight was pathetic in the extreme. They were all wailing in the minor key the same sound – o Tormod.

Friday Sept 27th 1907

Went into William's house where there was an assembly of women. There I heard the astounding intelligence that Annie MacQueen, daughter of Finlay, is to have a baby in a month or two, and that the father is our friend Donald

Gillies, son of poor Finlay Gillies. We are awfully sorry about it, and would never have believed it of the latter. Saw Annie MacQueen (one of the culprits) in bed in William's house, as her father put her out of the house last night and says that he will never allow her to darken his doors again.

Saturday May 23rd 1908

Another big boat came in. Who was this but a big Norwegian boat and our friend Mr Herlofson on board. We had a lovely day with him. We are going to Bunamhuinedor to see him on our return from south. A man and his wife from Harris and the wife's sister also came as guests to Hugh Gillies' house (to spy out the land & see if the sister wd. stay as Hugh's wife). The girl wasn't willin'!

Monday March 22nd 1909

Two boats left for Boreray to see about sheep etc. And Kate told me when she came to tidy my room that five men (Donald MacDonald, John Gillies, Neil MacKinnon, Norman MacQuien and his brother John) went to the Dun in William's boat. Kate had gone out of the room and my window was left open as the day was so lovely. All at once I heard the most terrible cries from the Dun & I called to Kate, who ran out and in turn gave the alarm up that something had happened at the Dun. Duine came from school in time to help old Angus, Finlay and Finlay MacQuien, and in a very short time they got across to the scene of whatever had happened. The suspense at home was awful; the women were all down & the anguished weeping and wailing I cannot describe. However, the boat came & our worst fears were realised; worse than we ever imagined. Donald MacDonald, Norman and John MacQuien were all drowned. Neil MacKinnon and John Gillies were rescued in a very exhausted condition. Donald MacDonald's body was found floating in the water, but poor Norman and John had gone down gripping each other. A beacon was lighted at Berenahake to make the men come home as it seems they purposed staying to kill gannets.

St Kilda was slipping slowly and inexorably towards its end. By 1920 the population had dropped to 64 of whom only 18 men could be regarded as of working age. When House No 4 went empty in 1917, everyone knew that it would never be inhabited again – a daily reminder to everyone that the community was on its way out. When the MacKinnons, who included most of the children on the island, began to consider emigration, the rest had to accept that they also would have to leave. It is easy to blame the government, the church, the nurse or anyone else you fancy, but we have to accept also that the gene pool of the island had become too restricted. Only one girl on the island was not a first cousin of all of the boys – and she was a second cousin!

I remember talking to one of the old Hiortaich about what it meant to him as a young man to leave the island, and his reply was that it meant he could have a girl-friend – actually he phrased it rather more succinctly! The question of inbreeding had been looked at in 1865 by Dr Mitchell in an article on Consanguineous Marriages:

There are 14 married couples on the island, being a fall from 129 at the census of 1851. In not one of these couples is the relationship between husband and wife that of full cousins. Not less than 5, however, of the 14 are marriages between second cousins. Of these five couples 54 children have been born, of whom 37 died in early infancy, leaving 17 alive. Of the 17 survivors it is distinctly stated that not one is either insane, imbecile, idiotic, blind, deaf, cripple, deformed or in any way defective in body or mind. With regard to the rest of the population only one insane person was found on the island, who is described as upwards of fifty years of age and of weak mind. Even this, of course, being 1 in 79, is far above the average for Scotland.

To allow for the lack of relationship he notes, there must have been at least two different MacKinnon families, two Gillieses and three MacDonalds, of whom at least one, and possibly more, families could have been of the original stock, in addition to one MacCrimmon, one MacQueen, one MacLeod and one Ferguson.

Health, or more accurately infant mortality, became a pressing issue in the mid to late 1800s. Infantile tetanus, sometimes referred to as trismus, was endemic all up and down the west coast of Scotland, Ireland and Iceland. '*Many infants die of a complaint called the five nights' sickness from their dying of it upon the fifth or sixth night; there are no instances of any who have been seized with it that escaped, nor has the nature of this uncommon disease as yet been fully comprehended.*' So wrote Rev. Donald MacDonald of Barvas, Lewis, in 1797 for the Statistical Account of Scotland. The same disease, reckoned in Hiort as eight-day sickness, caused the death of 13 out of the 23 children born between 1856 and 1865. In an article for the *Edinburgh Medical Journal* in 1865, Dr. Arthur Mitchell considered the probable causes:

Sixty years ago, in the Dublin Lying-In Hospital, every sixth child born there died within a fortnight after birth, and nineteen twentieths of these deaths were attributable to trismus. Dr Clarke blamed the ventilation, improved it, and the mortality fell at once from 1 in 6 to 1 in 19.3; while under further changes when Dr Collins was master, the whole deaths fell to 1 in 58½, and of that diminished mortality only one ninth resulted from trismus.

I made careful enquiry as to the mode of dressing the umbilical cord, but I did not find anything so exceptional in this matter as to lead me to suppose that it was in any way connected with the disease. In short, I can discover nothing which appears to me to be so probably the cause of this disease in St Kilda as the style of house in which the people live, and I am of the opinion that if their dwellings were improved, one result will be the extirpation of trismus.

Despite Dr. Mitchell's report, tetanus on Hiort only got worse. Between 1865 and 1875 out of twenty-six children, only 6 survived. To me one of the saddest things on St Kilda is the gravestone, now I believe rendered almost illegible by lichen, of – 'Finlay, the only son of Angus Gillies, died 1878 aged 20 years' – so sad because he was <u>not</u> the only son – his parents had had six previous children, all of whom had died of tetanus – and they had not even counted them! A child was not reckoned as really alive until the danger period was past, and only then would baby-clothes etc be prepared for them. As Fiddes reported – '*A St Kildan mother never thought, hitherto, of making any preparations for the new visitor. He or she was wrapped in a piece of blanket till the ninth or tenth day was over.*'

All sorts of suggestions were made for the cause of the trouble – one of the most lurid being the dressing of the baby's cord with rancid fulmar oil kept in the usual receptacle, the stomach of a gannet, but this was actually a comment by Dr Gibson, as late as 1926, that *if* such a routine was carried out, it *could* be the cause. Mitchell's suggestions were ignored as being much too mundane! Rev. Angus Fiddes could not accept that such deaths were necessary. He brought nurses from the mainland, but the Hiortaich women, ever distrustful of strangers, would not allow them at childbirth. So Fiddes went down to Glasgow himself for instruction by Professor Reid there in general cleanliness, the proper care of the cord, the use of iodoform and the need for new clean clothes for the new-born child – and no children died of tetanus after his return.

But still we have learned papers every so often giving this or that explanation of the St Kilda tetanus, as if it were specific to that island alone, and not endemic all over the west coast. The only special item about St Kilda tetanus was how long it took to be dealt with by the use of antiseptics. When they did arrive, it was too late – the population had fallen too low to be able to recover on its own, and what woman would be willing to marry and go to live on St Kilda? Well, actually one did! Ann MacLeod from Caolas Scalpaigh on Harris got married in 1912 to Ewen Gillies of Hiort. This is the same Ewen Gillies as Mrs MacLachlan mentioned as having had an unsuccessful visit from a potential wife from Harris 'on approval' as it were. Ewen and Ann came back to the island, where their daughter Mary Ann was born in 1915. Unfortunately Ewen was drowned in the following year. Ann later moved in with John MacDonald, whose wife had been deserted on the mainland, but in the report on the preparations for the evacuation she is at pains to stress that she was only there as a housekeeper!

In 1922 Lord Leverhulme tried to persuade the Hiortaich to move to his new village at Leverburgh, but only one family, the MacDonalds – the biggest family on the island – did so, and they were forced to move on to Stornoway after Leverhulme's death and the collapse of his plans for Harris. In 1928 Rev. Finlay MacQueen from Australia, a son of Malcolm who emigrated in 1852, came to Hiort and tried to persuade the remaining families to return with him to Australia. They still preferred to remain on Hiort, but two years later there was no longer any choice. The MacKinnon family, 10 out of the remaining 36 Hiortach, decided that they were going to leave, no matter what the others might wish – and there was no way that the remaining 26 could stay without them. Nurse Barclay and Dugald Munro, the missionary, helped them write a petition to the Government to be taken off the island. The ensuing official report highlighted the problems:

> The St Kildans are not crofters as is popularly supposed. Round the houses are the remains of crofts but it is many years since the crofts were cultivated as such, and almost the only produce now grown is potatoes and that apparently in a haphazard inexpert way, Even fishing is not now attempted on any scale worth considering, The present occupations of the islanders comprise the rearing and tending and shearing of sheep, the spinning of wool and the weaving of a rough kind of tweed, the knitting of socks and gloves, the collection of birds – mainly the fulmar – for food, the collection of birds' eggs for sale and, lastly, the exploitation of tourists. In the past the influence of Neil Ferguson, senior, has always prevented any definite action being taken. He is comparatively well off and would be quite content to remain on the island if he could be assured of a continuance of the profit the presence of the others brings him. Recently there have been distinct signs of a revolt against his domination.

On 29th August 1930, the *Harebell* took the remaining Hiortaich off the island, and the history of St Kilda as an indigenous community was at an end. Even at that moment, another book was being written, and Alasdair Alpin's MacGregor's *A Last Voyage to St Kilda,* a title carefully copied from Martin Martin, is an interesting account of how he made a nuisance of himself on that sad occasion! There has of course been no shortage of books since then, and I certainly could not comment on all, or even half of them! – but I think it fair to say that until recently there has been a lack of writings about the people of St Kilda and their family histories. David Quine has tried to remedy this in his *St Kilda Portraits* and *St Kilda Revisited* and my own *Croft History of St Kilda* gives the history of each family up to the evacuation.

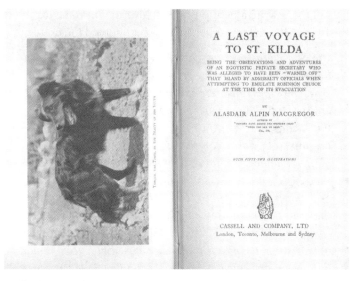

Half-title page of 'A Last Voyage to St Kilda' by Alasdair Alpin MacGregor

Calum Ferguson's *St Kilda Heritage*, and even more so its Gaelic version as *Hiort far na Laigh a' Ghrian* manages to import a light hearted touch to his gathering together of previous writings about St Kilda – no mean feat in what can so easily be a pessimistic history – and even better he includes songs and tunes from St Kilda. There is certainly a shortage of books in Gaelic about St Kilda, but then the same is true all through the Highlands and Islands – the Gael was not encouraged to write in his own tongue – and probably could not have found a publisher or printer if he had.

We have now two new books of reminiscences of Rev. Donald Gillies and Calum MacDonald, both of whom were brought up on St Kilda prior to the emigration, and so can add to our understanding of the last days of that community. But for most of the history of St Kilda, we still have to rely on writers from outside, some of whose impressions I have tried to catalogue in this talk.

Voices from St Kilda in the School of Scottish Studies Archives

Cathlin Macaulay

St Kilda has been written about at length, much of the time by those who have little inside knowledge of the place, the people or the language. Of the 700 or so publications, a couple were written by islanders themselves and a handful of others involve lengthy interviews with those who were living there. Few of those who have written about it have spent even a week on

Figure 1. Village Bay, 1938

Photo: Robert Atkinson (SSSA)

the island and there are hardly any books in Gaelic, the mother tongue of its inhabitants. This is, perhaps, not surprising given that few Gaelic speakers over the centuries have been schooled in their native language. However, this scenario raises many questions, not least of which is how accurate, how truthful, how real are these 700 or so accounts in depicting the particular way of life lived on the archipelago? Apart from credibility, the main question is why? Why have so many been moved to write about something of which they have so little first hand experience? The overall purpose of this conference was to deal with these questions and examine the historiography of St Kilda. The aim of this particular presentation was, in a sense, to redress the balance – to listen to the voices of St Kildan people – the 'insiders'.

The original presentation consisted of a collage of sound – stories, songs and accounts of life on the island. Ironically, in subsuming the audio to text here, we lose the texture of the voice, the very distinctive dialect, the intonation, the timbre, the rhythm, the emotion that was expressed through and along with the words. We lose the 'reality' that comes with the voice. I am not going to present 'a' narrative of life on St Kilda here. Rather, I will thread together a few of the pieces, the voices contained in recordings held in the School of Scottish Studies Archives, in the form of transcriptions. This will, I hope, give a flavour of the rich and varied material that is held in the Archives.

Archive holdings from St Kilda include audio, visual and textual material. The School was set up in 1951 to research, archive and publish material relating to the cultural life and traditions of Scotland and now comprises a Sound Archive, a Photographic Archive and a small Manuscript Archive along with a substantial library of publications – books and journals – many of which were donated by individual collectors. The Sound Archive holds over 13,000 fieldwork recordings including material from the Linguistic Survey of Scotland, which commenced in the late 1940s, and the Scottish Place-name Survey. There are, in addition, various donated collections, both from individuals and oral history projects. Some of the audio material on which the talk was based is now available on-line through the website Tobar an Dualchais/Kist o Riches (www.tobarandualchais.co.uk).

The earliest sound recordings relating to St Kilda were made in 1951. Donald MacQueen and Angus MacDonald were interviewed as part of the Gaelic Linguistic Survey by Fred Macaulay[1]. Along with the recorded interviews a standardised questionnaire was used comprising a word list from which phonetic transcriptions were made. The following year Calum Maclean talked to Donald Gillies and Kate Gillies as part of the fieldwork programme of the School of Scottish Studies. In 1961 the main series of recordings was made by John MacInnes in company with Iain Crawford. These include interviews with Donald MacQueen, his nephew Norman MacQueen, Lachlan MacKinnon and Neil Ferguson and later, in 1975, Lachlan MacDonald. These recordings contain some of the few first hand accounts of life on St Kilda by the islanders themselves. Many more interviews were undertaken with Lachie by David Clement from the 1970s until 1987 under the auspices of the Gaelic Linguistic Survey. Annabella MacLeod (nee MacDonald) was recorded in 1978. Most of these recordings are in Gaelic. Donated material, most of which is in English, includes recordings made by Billy Kay and Norman Chalmers for the seminal *Odyssey* series, first broadcast by the BBC in 1980. Lachie MacDonald and Neil Gillies participated along with Janet Chalmers, daughter of Christina MacQueen, Mary Cameron

---

1. See C Ó Dochartaigh (ed.), *Survey of the Gaelic Dialects of Scotland* (Dublin Institute for Advanced Studies, 5 vols. Dublin, 1994–1997).

who was there as a child, and various others, some of whom visited or stayed on the island after the evacuation.[2]

Sound recordings are complemented by material in the Photographic Archive. Ian Whitaker took photographs of buildings and structures during his visit of 1957 when he accompanied D R MacGregor of the Geography Department at Edinburgh University who, prior to the setting up of the military base, was undertaking a geographical survey of the island.[3] Donated material includes glass slides by R C MacLeod of MacLeod taken in 1905 and the Lamont Collection from Dr David Christie who was the locum between 1910 and 1912. We also hold the Robert Atkinson Collection. Atkinson visited St Kilda a number of times. He described his first visit, in 1938, in the book *Island Going*[4]. By this time the island had been bought by the Marquis of Bute who had, somewhat ironically, turned it into a bird sanctuary. Atkinson was there for three weeks at the same time as Neil Gillies, Mrs Gillies and Finlay MacQueen.

Most of the contributors were quite far on in years when they were recorded. By then they would have been away for a longer time than they lived on the island. A wide range of topics was discussed. Information on everyday life on St Kilda includes areas such as food, fowling, housing and buildings, crops and cultivation, animal husbandry, weather, telling the time, fishing, boats, peat cutting, wool work, tweed making, rents, factors, religion and church going, schooling, wedding and funeral customs, interaction with visitors and the so-called St Kilda Parliament. Place-names, stories and events also feature.

2. See Billy Kay (ed.), *Odyssey: Voices From Scotland's Recent Past* (Polygon, 1980).

3. *Scottish Studies* IV, 1 – 48 (School of Scottish Studies, University of Edinburgh, 1960).

4. Robert Atkinson, *Island Going* (Birlinn, 2008).

Figure 2. Robert Atkinson, Finlay MacQueen, Mrs Gillies, Neil Gillies, 1938

The island is most renowned for its bird life today and the islanders for their fowling skills. Roderick Campbell, from Bragar in Lewis, went to St Kilda in May 1901 at the age of nineteen to work as the schoolteacher for a year. As a Gaelic speaker and Leodhsach he had some insight into island life. He describes the 'bird year':

They went for the fulmar in August and September. I think the fulmar started at the very same time as the grouse on the moors … I think it was about the 12th of August. That's the fulmars. But supposing it was now the gannets or their eggs they wanted. Well that would be the month of April. And supposing it was the puffins – it was the month of April too. And when they went for the puffins – that was for snaring the puffins that they went, with a rod out, 12 to 15 feet long, with a noose at the end of it made of twine or gut.

39

And then this noose was big enough for the puffin to put his head into it and then you had a tug at the rod and the noose tightened round the neck and then you pulled the bird towards you and wring it by the neck, put it in a bag and then out again with the rod for the next one ... They plucked them and salted them and used them for meat in the winter time. They did the same thing with the fulmars. They did the same thing with the guillemots too and the razorbills but they weren't of course so common as the puffins. The puffins simply covered the ground you know ... the rocks were black with the puffins.[5]

Dogs would also be used to chase puffin from their burrows. The recordings contain detailed, ethnological accounts of fowling expeditions made by participants Donald MacQueen and Norman MacQueen who were initiated in cliff climbing skills whilst in their teens. These were required for the fulmar hunt, a communal activity which took place whilst the birds were still fledglings and unable to fly away. The rocks were divided into shares for each family annually – lots were cast using matches or feathers. The men set off in the morning and worked until evening. Two men generally worked together. A rope was tied round the middle of the man who went down the cliff, the other end held by the man at the top. Another rope was fixed to a post. The birds were killed in their nests. Norman MacQueen describes places where the cliff was so sheer you were just hanging except for a toe hold in the rock. The fowler carried about twenty birds, tied in bundles on his back and shoulders, up the cliff using both hands on the fixed rope while the man at the top hauled. He might go up and down twenty times in a day. When the evening came the

---

5. Roderick Campbell recorded by Eric Cregeen. Transcription by Cathlin Macaulay (School of Scottish Studies Archives, SA1958.192).

Photo: Robert Atkinson (SSSA)

Figure 3. Finlay MacQueen snaring puffins, 1938

birds were taken back to the village. The oil was squeezed out through the beak into a can and then the birds were plucked and cleaned, split, salted and put in hogsheads for the winter, rather like herring with a layer of rough salt followed by a layer of birds. Both men and women worked sometimes until two or four in the morning.

In contrast, gannets were taken at night. When the rocks were white you knew the gannets were there all night. Two boats would go across to Stac Lì in the twilight and wait until it was

41

dark, so dark you couldn't see your hand. A rope would be tied to a bolt on the rock. The fowlers would leap ashore (the sea was too rough for the boat to land) and climb up a narrow path in the rock while the birds were asleep. Silence was paramount. Not a word would be said and communication involved tugging a rope between the men. The sentry bird would be taken. There were two birds in each nest and you had to take one without waking the other and kill it by twisting its neck, or take the two birds at the same time. At dawn the birds were thrown into the sea from where the boats would pick them up. Any noise disturbed the birds and led to severe peckings. The birds were divided into portions for each family.

Guillemots were caught by climbing down the rock to their nests on a crevice. The fowler would crouch down with his back to the rock and the sea booming under him and catch them as they came back at dawn. If you put one to your breast the others would fly towards the white spot. Once you had a bundle they were hauled up by the man on top.[6]

The birds' flesh provided food – soup made with oatmeal and dried salt meat for the winter months. Neil Gillies mentions a particular fondness for shearwater soup. Young fulmar could be fried – no extra oil was required. Oil was used at one time for the crusie lamps and, along with the feathers, used to pay the rent. The eggs were collected and used for food (except for gulls' eggs). Eggs were also blown and sold to tourists.

Fowling and fishing provided much of the subsistence for the people on St Kilda. They also grew crops – barley and oats and later potatoes, cabbage, turnips and rhubarb – and kept cows and sheep. Sheep's milk was used to make cheese and their fleece

---

6. English synopsis from information given by Norman MacQueen and Donald MacQueen to John MacInnes (School of Scottish Studies Archives, SA1961.18, 20, 21).

was an important part of the economy, providing the means of making the famous St Kildan tweed. Tweed was sold to pay the rent and provided cash for sugar, tea and other bought provisions. It went to the factor, and latterly to A G Ferguson who had left the island and set up a business in Glasgow. He returned regularly and also provided a staging post for those who left, providing accommodation and helping them to find work. Wool work was done in the winter as Lachie MacDonald describes here:

Ach 's e obair a bha truagh a bhith anns an àite bha sin. Cha robh mòran tìde agad dhuit fhèin ann an dòigh mar sin. O 's dòcha lathaichean dheth, ach even 's a' gheamhradh bha thu trang a sin. Bha thu 's a' gheamhradh bha thu mach fhad's a bha … ma bha an latha goirid ann. Bha thu mach 's a' mhonadh a' coimhead air na beothaichean 's gnothaichean dhen t-seòrsa sin: caoraich 's … Bha thu sin a' tighinn dhachaidh 's dòcha nuair bhiodh i fàs dorcha. Bha thu 'faotainn do dhìnneir, no rud sam bith, dè bha 'dol – tì. Bha thu 'ga do ghlanadh fhèin. Bha thu 'suidhe sin 's bha thu tòiseachdainn air sgrìobadh cards a bha siod 'mix-eadh a' chlòimh 's gnothaichean dhan t-seòrsa sin. Bha thu ga chur ann an rolls mar bha e 'tighinn a mach as a' mhuileann 's bha cuidheall … cuidheall snìomh a sin. Bha thu sin a' tòiseachdainn air … Well, 's e na boirionnaich daonnan a bha 'dèanamh an snìomh. Agus bha sin a' dol air fad na h-oidhche, 's dòcha bhiodh gu uair 's a' mhaduinn, dà uair 's a' mhaduinn. Nuair a gheibheadh tu sin dèanamh bha thu – 's a stanard deas 's a h-uile càil – bha thu, mar a their sinne ris deirbh (deilbh) a sin. Chan eil fhios agamsa do thuig thu sin. 'S e na flat board 's … pineachan a siod 's pineachan a seo 's bha thu 'cur … 'dol suas 'us sìos a sin. Agus bha … Sin an gno … Bha e particular sin gos am faigheadh tu e, gos a chur a sin. Bha thu 'ga chur dhan bheart … … 'g a

*fhigheadh. Bha thu 'g a chur ann an òrdugh air son a dhol
g' a fhigheadh. 'S bha thu sin a' tòiseachdainn air figheadh.
Agus 's e do chasan 's do làmhan. Cha robh nì mechanic a
sin. 'S e do làmhan 's do chasan a bha thu 'g obair.*

∞

*But it was hard work being in that place. You did not have
much time to yourself in a way, like that. Oh, perhaps there
were days off, but even in the winter you were busy there.
In the winter you were out as long as … since the day was
short … you were out on the hill looking after the animals
and things like that – sheep – and … you would then come
home perhaps when it was getting dark. You would get your
dinner, or something, whatever was going – tea … You would
clean yourself. Then you would sit down, and you would then
start scraping with these cards, mixing the wool, and tasks of
that kind. You would make it into rolls, as it came out of
the mill. And there was a wheel, a spinning-wheel there. You
would then begin to … Well, it was always the women who
did the spinning. And that went on all night, perhaps till one
o'clock in the morning or two o'clock in the morning. When
you got that done you would … and the yardstick ready and
every thing … you would (as we call it) warp that. I do not
know if you understood that? It is the flatboard, and pegs
here and pegs there, and you would put … you would go up
and down on that. And it was … that was the problem … it
was particular, that, until you got it right, to put it there. You
were to put it in the loom to weave it. You would put it in
order for weaving. And then you began weaving. And it was
a matter of feet and hands. There was nothing mechanical
there, it was your hands and feet you used.*[7]

---

7. Lachie MacDonald recorded by David Clement. Transcription
by Peggy McClement, translation by Cathie Scott (SSSA, GLS959).

Figure 4. Mrs Gillies, 1938

The life was hard and work unremitting. People pulled together to survive. The evacuation of St Kilda was, perhaps, inevitable. The First World War had shown young people a different way of life. Due both to emigration and various accidents which took the lives of those fishing and fowling, there were ever fewer young able-bodied men. It became impossible to sustain the community, particularly as no adequate health or service infrastructure was put in place by the Government. While the young were glad to leave, the older people were very sad. One

45

of the aspects that people missed when they left was the close community network – they were widely dispersed rather than settled in the one place. Those that were interviewed were very aware of the misrepresentations of their way of life, particularly in relation to icons such as the St Kilda Parliament, the Lover's Stone, the four-horned sheep...

One of the many myths and misrepresentations that the people share with their Hebridean neighbours is that the influence of strict Presbyterianism essentially killed the traditional arts and beliefs of those who lived there. As Donald Meek makes clear, traditional belief and beliefs related to the Church could exist side by side in St Kilda as in the rest of the Hebrides.[8] It is true that the people were renowned for their psalm singing but that does not preclude other singing occasions. Lachie MacDonald indicates that women sang while waulking the cloth and various contributors to the Archives recollect songs learned from St Kildan people. Jessie Ann MacLeod of Harris mentions that she first heard the song, *Do dha shuil bheag bhiorach gam choimhead troimh'n toll*[9] from someone from St Kilda. They used to come to the whaling station in Harris before the First World War and when they came they would call in at the houses and would begin to sing:

> *'S nuair a thigeadh iad air tìr bhiodh iad a' tadhal a's na taighean agus 's màite nuair a bhiodh iad nan suidhe 's a'leigeil dhiu an sgìos, gun tòisicheadh iad air seinn, direach duanag dha na bhiodh ac' a's an eilean.*[10]

---

8. See Donald Meek's conference paper: Towards a Re-examination of the Role of Church and Faith in St Kilda.

9. Your two wee bright eyes watching me through the hole.

10. Jessie Ann MacLeod, Harris, recorded by James Ross. Transcription and translation by Morag MacLeod (School of Scottish Studies Archives, SA1957.93).

The well-known song *Mo ghaol òigear a' chùil duinn* was composed by Mòr (Marion) Gillies of St Kilda, and is still extant in the oral tradition in the Uists. Mòr met and fell in love with a visitor to the island, one of the Campbells of Islay, a forebear of the collector John Frances Campbell (Iain Og Ile) according to the Reverend William Matheson from North Uist who has contributed many songs to the Archives[11]. Mòr eventually came to live in North Uist and from there went to Skye. Alexander Carmichael who had collected versions of *Mo ghaol òigear a' chùil duinn* met people who had come across her and learned that:

> *The composer of this song was known in the long island and in Skye as Mòr Hirteach. She had a marvellously beautiful face and features with an abundance [of] brown golden hair. She composed several songs and sang them to appreciative audiences. She had a beautiful liquid voice with this child like St Kilda lisp. She was simple, guileless and unaffected and easily induced to sing her own songs and tell her own history.*

She is described further as 'leannan falaich'[12] to Campbell of Islay.

The version of the song transcribed here was recorded from Mary Munro of South Uist who learned it from her mother as a song to accompany spinning.

---

11.   Rev. William Matheson had various sources for this song – his mother and his aunt knew it and he also had a version from Colina MacRury, daughter of the Reverend John MacRury.

12.   EUL CW MS 244, fos.325,328 (Carmichael Watson Collection, Edinburgh University Library). See also: Domhnall Uilleam Stiùbhart, 'Alasdair MacGilleMhìcheil: Fear-cruinneachaidh òrain ri linn nan 1860an' in Ruairí Ó hUiginn (ed.), *Foinn agus Focail: Léachtaí Cholm Cille XL* (Maynooth: An Sagart, 2010), 133.

Mo ghaol òigear a' chùil duinn

*Mo ghaol òigear a' chùil duinn air na ghabh mi loinn 's mi
òg*
Dhùraiginn dhut pòg san anmoch ged robh càch ga
sheanchas oirnn
*Mo ghaol òigear a' chùil duinn air na ghabh mi loinn 's mi
òg.*

Gura mise tha gu gallach, dìreadh 's a' teàrnadh a'
ghleannain
Chan fhaic mi tighinn mo leannan, fear gun sgar an cainnt
a bheòil.

Gura mise tha fo uallach on a thàinig an duin'uasal
Cnot de ribinn air a ghualainn – cumaidh siud mo ghruag
air dòigh.

Ged a gheibhinn fhìn am Muileach 's na bh'aige de stòras
 uile,
B'annsa gìomanach a' ghunna chuireadh fuil air damh na
 cròic.

Ged a thog iad oirnn na breugan, gu robh mo chriosan ri
 gèirigh
Giùlainidh sinn sin gu h-eutrom; ò, cha dèan e eucail
 oirnn.

Sguiridh mi shùgradh nan gillean, ged is math leam a
 bhith mire;
Bhon tha 'n Caimbeulach gam shireadh, cha tèid mi do
 ghion tha beò.

My love the brown-haired youth with whom I fell in love
 when I was young
I'd wish to kiss you late at night, even if everyone talked
 about us.
My love the brown-haired youth…

I am impatient climbing and descending the glen
I can't see my sweetheart coming, he is flawless in his talk.

I am anxious, indeed, since the nobleman came, a ribbon
 knotted on his shoulder –
That will hold my hair in place.

Even if I were to catch the Mull man, with all his wealth,
Better would be the huntsman with his gun, who would
 draw blood on the antlered stag.

Although they slandered us, that my waist belt was rising,
We'll endure that lightly, it will not harm us.

I'll give up courting, although I do like flirting,
Since Campbell is pursuing me I shan't go to anyone else.[13]

There are various tales in the archive which indicate that storytelling among people from St Kilda, as in the rest of the Hebrides at that time, was strong. The following tale, Dùgan is Fearchar Mòr – Dugan and Big Farquhar, comes from Norman MacQueen. This is a story that was known and told by practically all of those who were interviewed – each of the tellings having slight variations.

Dùgan is Fearchar Mòr

Dùgan is Fearchar Mòr: bhiodh iad a' falbh 'na h-Eileanan Flannach a mharbhadh chaorach – a ghoid chaorach agus 'gan toir leotha Hirte. Agus co-dhiù, là bha seo, dh'fhalbh iad a mhullach na beinneadh, Dùgan is Fearchar. Agus bha teampull ann an t-Hirte fo'n talamh far am biodh daoine teicheadh ma thigeadh an nàmhaid. Agus bha an dorus cho caol air agus chan fhaigheadh sibh a staigh ann mara deidheadh sibh a staigh ann air an oir. Agus dh'fhalbh an dà bhodach a bha seo, là bha seo, mhullach na beinneadh agus thòisich iad ri eubhach à mullach na beinneadh gu robh na soitheachan-cogadh … cogadh a's a' Chaolas Bhoighreach agus a chuile duine aca dhol dh'an teampull. Well, dh'fhalbh na daoine bochd air fad dh'an teampull a bha seo agus 'se rinn mo liagh (sic) ach thòisich iad ri buain fraoch; bhuain

---

13.   Mary Munro, South Uist, recorded by Donald Archie MacDonald. Transcription and translation by Morag MacLeod (SSSA, SA1966.09). In verse 3, Morag MacLeod notes that a more common text goes 'Gura mise tha gu h-uallach …/ I am proud indeed….' There are several versions of this song in the SSSA by singers including Effie Monk, Kate MacDonald and William Matheson. It has been published in the *MacDonald Collection of Gaelic Poetry*, Revs A and A MacDonald (Inverness, 1911), and in *Songs of Gaelic Scotland*, Anne Lorne Gillies (ed.) (Birlinn, 2005).

*iad boitean a (sic) fraoch a' fear agus thug iad leotha am
boitean a' fear air an gualainn is thàinig iad dhachaigh.*

*Is bha na daoin a's an teampull. Ach bha rùm gu leòr
gu h-iseal a's an teampull. Agus nuair a thàinig iad a nuas
a [?] cha do rinn iad càil ach chuir iad am boitean ris an
dorus agus chuir iad maidse leis agus thac iad a chuile duine
riamh bha 'san àite. Ach fhuair aon nighean – bha i còig
bliadhna diag – fhuair ise mach a measg a' cheò a bha seo
agus chaidh i ann an uamha dh'fhalach gus an dàinig am
bàta [... ...]. Agus coma co-dhiù là bha seo an dèidh dhiu na
daoine mharbhadh, chaidh iad a ghabhail ceum – Dùgan is
Fearchar. Agus ... 'A ghoistidh! a ghoistidh!, as an dala fear
ris an fhear eile, 'tha mi faotainn àileadh teine seo!' 'Ho! isd
amadain! Chan 'eil', as eisein, 'ach teine dh'fhàg thu as do
dheaghaidh.' Agus dè bh'ann ach bha an nighean a theich
bha i fo'n a' chreag a bha seo fòtha agus cha do rinn i càil ach
a h-aodach a chuir ma mhullach na poiteadh a bh'aic air an
teine le biadh fiach gun cumadh i an ceò gun a dhol a suas.
'Och', as eisein, 'a ghoistidh, ghoistidh, 'se an teine a dh'fhàg
sinn as ar n-deaghaidh'.*

*Well, dh'fhalbh iad an uairsin is ghabh iad ceum agus là
airne mhàireach thàinig a' soitheach a bha seo – soitheach a'
bhàillidh. Agus bha nighean, bha i a's an toll a bha seo, cha
dàinig i mach leis an eagal agus dh'fhan i a's an toll gos a robh
am bàta beag gu bhith aig a' chidhe agus nuair a bha am bàta
gun a bhith aig a' chidhe, thàinig i mach as an toll agus chaidh
an dithis acasan a sìos a choinneachadh an eathar, 'eil thu
faicinn? Agus nuair a mhothaich iad dh'an nighean, as an dala
fear ris an fhear eile, "S fhearr dhuinn falbh agus a marbhadh'.
Well, cha d'fhuair iad ... cha d'fhuair iad an t-seansa ... cha
d'fhuair iad an t-seansa marbhadh. Chaidh iad ... leum na
daoine mach as an eathar is fhuair iad greim air an nighean a
bha seo agus dh'inns an nighean dhiu a' naidheachd.*

51

Well, rugadh air an dala fear aca – rugadh air Fearchar
agus chuireadh e Stac an Aramair a measg nan eòin agus
chuireadh Dùgan a Shòaigh, an eilean eile tha an iar air
Hirte, measg nan caorach agus a measg nan ian. Well, a'
fear a chuir iad a Stac an Aramair, ghearr e as deaghaidh
an eathair agus chaidh a bhàthadh – cha do thog iad idir e –
ghearr e mach air a' mhuir is leig iad leis gun do bhàsaich
e. Ach Dùgan, chaidh a chuir a Shòaigh agus bha e ann
bliadhnachan beò; bhiodh e 'g ithe nan caorach is ag ithe
nan eòin. Than a h-asnaichean aige fhathasd ann a shiod:
dh'fhiach mi fhèin na h-asnaichean 'na mo làimh.

∽

Dugan and Big Farquhar: they used to go to the Flannan
Islands to kill sheep – to steal sheep and bring them back
to St Kilda. Well, one day they went up to the top of the hill,
Dugan and Farquhar. And there was a temple in St Kilda,
underground, where people used to flee if an enemy came.
The door was so narrow that you could not get in unless
you entered sideways. And these two fellows went to the
top of the hill one day and began to shout from the top of
the hill that there were warships in the Kyle of Boreray and
everyone to go to the temple. Well, all the poor people went
to this temple and what did my bold lad(s) do but begin
to cut heather; each of them cut a bundle of heather and
carried his bundle on his shoulder and they came home.

The people were in the temple, but there was plenty of
room down inside it. And when they (the two men) came ...
they immediately placed the bundle against the doorway and
they lit it with a match and they choked every single person
in the place. But one girl managed – she was fifteen years
of age – she managed to get out in the smoke there and she
went to a cave to hide until the ship arrived [... ...]. At any
rate, one day after they had killed the people, they went out

for a stroll – Dugan and Farquhar. And … 'My friend!' said one of them to the other, 'I get the smell of fire here!' 'Oh quiet, you fool! It is only the fire that you have left after you'. What was it but the girl who escaped; she was underneath the rock below them and at once she placed her clothes over the top of the pot that she had on the fire with food in it, so as to keep the smoke from ascending. 'Och my friend', said he, 'it is the fire that we left after us'.

Well, they went off then and they took a stroll and the following day the ship came – the factor's ship. And the girl, she was in the hole there; she did not come out through fear and she remained in the hole until the small boat was almost at the pier, and when the boat was almost at the pier she came out of the hole and the two men went down to meet the boat, do you see? When they observed the girl, one said to the other, 'We had better go and kill her'. Well, they did not get a chance to kill her. The men leapt out of the boat and they caught hold of the girl, and the girl told them the tale.

Well, one of them was seized – Farquhar was seized and put out on to Stac an Aramair among the birds, and Dugan was sent to Soay – on another island west of St Kilda – among the birds and among the sheep. The man whom they sent to Stac an Aramair, he jumped after the boat and was drowned: they did not pick him up – he jumped into the sea and they left him until he died. But Dugan, he was sent to Soay and he was there alive for years: he used to eat the sheep and the birds. His ribs are there still; I myself have handled the ribs.[14]

---

14. Norman MacQueen recorded by John MacInnes (SSSA, SA1961.19). Transcription and translation republished from *Scottish Studies* V, 215–219 (School of Scottish Studies, University of Edinburgh, 1961).

Photo: Robert Atkinson (SSSA)

Figure 5. Stac an Armainn, 1938

Another event in which the island's people were just about wiped out was the smallpox epidemic of the 1720s.

What happened … it was in August and there was only the factor boat that called from Skye to the island. And they must have got smallpox from maybe some of the crew – through that boat anyway. That's the only way they could have got it. And at that time, that's the time they used to go and do the guga – and there was eight or nine – a boatload of the men were on one of the stacks. And this smallpox broke out on the island and every one of them was dead except one man and it's him that buried the rest. He was the only one alive as far as the story goes. And the men were on this stack. They had no clothes, no food all the winter til the next May til the boat came from Skye again and went to the island. And this was the only man they got there and he told them about the rest being on this island but they thought they would be all

dead. And they went across there and they were all living.
They kept themselves alive with hooks, catching fish on the
rocks. [They were on] Stac an Armainn – just a rock! On
that stack. They kept themselves alive with fish til the birds
came in the springtime and they were catching the birds.[15]

At this point the island was re-settled by people from Skye,
Berneray, Harris and the Uists – as indicated by the common
surnames of Ferguson, MacQueen, Gillies, MacDonald,
MacKinnon, MacCrimmon.

In many tales and songs the sea is a highway bringing
welcome and less welcome visitors. For a long time, regular
boats to St Kilda were rare and were expected only once or twice
a year. The island was very isolated and an ideal place on which
to get someone out of the way. Lady Grange was incarcerated
there by her husband who feared that she would reveal his
Jacobite sympathies. She is reputed to have sent messages out
to sea, pleading for rescue. The so-called St Kilda mailboat
appears to be an invention of visitor and journalist, John Sands
who in 1876, 'made a minature ship and put a letter in her hold,
in the hope that she might reach some place where there was
a post office, being anxious to let my friends know that I was
alive, and also to let the public know that Macleod had broken
his promise to send provisions to the people, and that we were
all in want…'.[16] He made another to call for help when a group
of Austrian mariners were shipwrecked and stranded on the
island. The captain 'brought me a life-buoy belonging to the lost
ship, and said he intended to send it off. I suggested that another
bottle should be tied to it, with a note enclosed to the Austrian

---

15.   Neil Ferguson recorded by John MacInnes (SSSA, SA1961.22).
16.   George Sands, *Out of the World or Life in St Kilda* (Maclachlan
and Stewart, Edinburgh, 1878), 109.

Consul, and that a small sail should be erected. This was done and the life-buoy was thrown into the sea, and went away slowly before the wind'.[17] It worked, landing in Orkney nine days later from where it was forwarded and a boat was sent to take the stranded sailors home. The mailboat became a source of endless fascination to visitors. Often islanders were asked to make one and send it out. Donald MacQueen describes this process. They took a good deal of work.

St Kilda Mail

Chan fhaigheadh tu litir … fad a' gheamhraidh ann an t-Hirte. Chan fhaiceadh tu soitheach air do dhà shùil. Tha cuimhne agamsa nach fhaiceadh tu soitheach … o dheireadh an t-samhraidh chun an ath shamhradh. Nam biodh dìth ort dh'fheumadh tu … Abair gu robh thusa … 'na do chroitear ann an t-Hirte agus gu robh teaghlach agad 's gun do ruith thu mach as a' bhiadh … bhiodh càch a' toir dhuit na chumadh beò thu gus an tigeadh soitheach.

Well, 'se bhiodh iad a' dèanamh ach craicionn caorach … air a chur ann an cairte-ciù … Dh'fhàgadh tu fad seachduin e ann an cairte-ciù. Agus chuireadh tu sin air bòrd e gus shretch-eadh tu mach e. Shlaodadh tu mach e, ga dhèanamh cho mòr 's a b'urrainn dhuit.

Iain MacAonghuis: Dìreach 'ga shlaodadh le ur làmhan, an ann?

Domhnall MacCuinn: Chan ann. Chan ann. Bha thu 'ga shlaodadh, 'ga chur air bòrd. Mar gun cuireadh tu air an dorus ann a shin e, 'ga shlaodadh a mach, 'cur tàirnnean ann … 'ga fhosgladh a mach. Well, 'nuair a bhiodh e agad fad seachduin … mar sin, bha e tioram. Bha thu 'dèanamh

17.   Ibid., 116–117.

buta dheth. Bha thu 'cur ceann fiodh air, agus 'ga cheangal le
ròpa timchioll air. Agus bha toll a's a cheann aige 's bha thu
'ga shèideadh 's cur làn gaoithe ann … Toll mar gum biodh
toll gimleid agad ann agus tu 'ga shèideadh le do bheul. Agus
a' cur a sin … bìdeag de ròpa ann, 'stad … 'toir stad air a'
ghaoth tighinn as. Well, chumadh tu e fad seachduin no fad
ceithir-là-deug gus am faiceadh tu 'robh e 'cumail na gaoithe.
Bha thu a' dèanamh a sin sgoth … pìos de phlanga, mu …
throigh a dh'fhad, no mu throigh gu leth a dh'fhad. 'S bha
thu 'dèanamh toiseach oirre mar gum biodh soitheach ann.
IM: Dìreach 'ga 'dèanamh biorach?
DM: Ai. Bha thu 'dèanamh toiseach oirre mar gum biodh
soitheach. 'S bha thu 'dèanamh an deireadh aice mar a
chitheadh tu deireadh soithich … Bha am planga ceithir
òirlich an leud, mu thrì òirlich a thighead. Bha thu le geilb,
bha thu 'cladhach toll a's a' mheadhon aice airson siuga beag
a dhol ann leis na litrichean … Cha robh stamp … Chan
fhaigheadh tu stamp ann. Dh'fheumadh tu an t-airgiod a
chur ann.

Well, 'nuair a rinn thu an toll a bh'ann a sheo, an cèaban
a bh'ann a sheo, bha thu 'cur cover air. Agus bha thu 'ga
dhèanamh nach deidheadh uisge 'na bhroinn. Agus bha thu
sgrìobhadh … bha thu 'gearradh a's an fhiodh air uachdar …
'St. Kilda Mail. Please open'. 'S bha thu 'ceangal na long a
bh'ann a sheo ris a' bhuta le pìos de ròpa no pìos de wire –
wire tana. Bha thu 'toir toll … a's a long, a's an toiseach aice …
bìdeag bheag os cionn uisge. Bha thu 'dèanamh toll gimleid
ann. Bha thu 'feitheamh a' cheud latha 's a' gheamhradh
nuair a bhiodh stoirm de ghaoth … an iar-dheas. An
iar 's an iar-dheas. Nuair a bhiodh a' ghaoth cha mhòr
a' toir as nan taighean bha thu 'dol a sìos leis … chun a'
cheidhe 's ga thilgeil a mach air a' mhuir 's cha robh an còrr
mu dheoghainn. Cha robh thu 'ga fhaicinn tuilleadh. Na

maireadh a' ghaoth, na maireadh i trì latha bhiodh e air an tìr-mhòr. Cha bhiodh fhios agad-sa na bhuail e air tìr-mhòr no de'd a bh'ann.

Bha … Ann a's t-samhradh bha a' Hebrides a' dol le uaislean gu Hirte. Bha seana bhodach mòr … a's an sgothaidh a' dol a staigh … 'S ann le ferry a bha iad 'ga chur … a toir nan uaislean gu tìr. Dh'fhoighneachd e dhomhsa. 'Chuala mi uamhas,' ors esan, 'timchioll air … air St. Kilda Mail.' Ors esan, 'B'fheàrr leam gum faighinn fhèin fear aca.'

'Och,' ors mise, 'tha e furasda gu leòir dhuit fear fhaotainn.'

'Bheil?' ors esan. 'Tha mi airson fhaotainn,' ors esan, 'mar a tha e. Am buta 's an long.'

Agus … 'Well,' orsa mise, 'ma bheir thusa dhomh-sa an address agad gheibh thu…' Bha e ann an Lunnainn. 'S ann a bha e 'fuireach. Orsa mise, 'Ma bheir thu dhomh-sa an address gheibh thu … chur thugad.'

'Am faigh?' ors esan.

'O gheibh.'

'Well,' ors esan, 'pàidhidh mise thu.'

'Och,' orsa mise, 'chan eil fhios agam-se dè na bhitheas e,' orsa mise, 'dol a Lunnainn. 'S chan eil fhios'am,' orsa mise, 'am faigh thu e … ged a thilginn-sa a mach air a mhuir e. B'urra dhuit,' orsa mise. 'bruidhinn air a sin 'nuair … gheibh thu e.'

Co-dhiù bha bràthair dhomh-sa … Dh'fhalbh sinn agus rinn sinn am buta. Rinn…

'Dè,' ors esan, 'tha thu 'g iarraidh,' ors esan, 'airson do dhragh?'

Cha robh fhios'am de'd a theirinn ris. 'Och,' orsa mise, 'nì not an gnothach.'

He says, 'What? Not,' ors esan, 'Cha deanadh sin,' ors esan, 'do dhragh.'

'Och nì,' orsa mise. Och, dheanadh tu ann an dà uair an uaireadar e. Dhèanadh tu ann an dà uair no ann an trì e easy, ach gum biodh e o thòisicheadh tu air gus am biodh tu deis bheireadh e barrachd is … dà uair, eadar a chur ann an cairte-ciù 's gnothach dhen t-seòrsa sin. Ach co-dhiù rinn sinn am buta co-dhiù. Thàinig stoirm de ghaoth an iar-dheas, stoirm a' toir as nan taighean. Bha am buta dèanta 's dh'fhalbh mise sìos leis … chun a' cheidhe. Thilg mi mach air a' mhuir e 's chan fhaca mi an ath shealladh. Cha robh an còrr mu dheoghainn 's cha robh soitheach ri fhaicinn.

An ceann seachduin no ceithir-là-deug thàinig trawler a ghabhail fasgadh a staigh dhan bhàgh 's gaoth an iar-dheas ann. Dh'fhalbh sinne mach thuice. Agus ors esan, 'Cò chuir,' ors esan, 'mail Hirte,' ors esan, 'cò chuir air falbh e?'

O thuirt iad ris gur e mise a chuir air falbh e.

'Cha tug e,' ors esan, 'ach trì latha,' ors esan, 'gus do rànaig e Sealtainn.'

Trì latha … Bha pìos a's a' phàipear mu dheoghainn.

An ath shamhradh thàinig litir on a' bhodach a bh'ann a seo … à Lunnainn, 'toir taing dhomh … gun d'fhuair e am buta leis an long. Bha e sgrìobhte le ticket a bha 'na bhroinn. Am broinn an t-siuga … an address aige a chuir … a' phostadh air falbh. Nis, cha chuala mi riamh dè na phàidh e air no càil ach thuirt e gun d'fhuair e e. Gun d'fhuair e e.

∾

You wouldn't get a letter … all winter in St Kilda. There wouldn't be a ship to be seen. I remember that you wouldn't see a ship … from the end of the summer until the next summer. If you were in need you would have to … Say you were a crofter in St Kilda and you had a family and that you ran out of food … the others would give you enough to keep you alive until a ship came.

Well what would they do but put a sheepskin in tan-bark. … You left it a whole week in the bark. And then you put it on a board so that you could stretch it out. You pulled it out, to make it as big as you could.

John MacInnes: Just pulling it with your hands?

Donald MacQueen: No. No. You stretched it, fixing it on a board. Say you put it on that door there, stretching it out, putting nails in … … to open it out. Well, when you had had it for a whole week … like that, it would be dry. You made a skin float of it. You would fit it with a wooden stopper, and you would tie rope round that. And there was a hole in the stopper and you blew into it and filled it full of air. You had a hole like a gimlet hole in it and you blew it up with your mouth. And you then put … a bit of rope in, stopping … to stop the air coming out. Well, you kept it for a whole week or a whole fortnight until you saw that it was holding the air. Then you made a boat … a piece of plank, about a foot long, or about a foot and a half long. And you made the bows of it as though it were a ship.

JM: Just making it pointed?

DM: Aye, you made a bow on it like a ship. And you made the stern as you would see the stern of a ship … The plank was four inches broad, about three inches thick. With a chisel … you scooped out a hole in the centre of it for a little jar to go in with the letters … You couldn't get a stamp. You had to put money in it.

Well, … when you made this hole, this cabin, you put a cover over it. And you made it watertight. And you wrote … You carved in the wood on the top … 'St Kilda Mail. Please open'. And you tied this boat to the float with a piece of rope or a piece of wire – thin wire. You made a hole … in the bow of the boat … a little bit above the waterline. You made a gimlet hole. You waited for the first winter day when there was a … southwest gale. West-southwest. When the wind was so strong that the houses almost took off you went down to the pier with it and threw it out in the sea and that was that. You didn't see it again. If the gale lasted three days it would reach the mainland. You wouldn't know if it had reached the mainland or what had happened.

Yes … in the summer the Hebrides went to St Kilda with gentry. There was an old gentleman … in the boat going ashore. It was by a ferry they put … brought the gentry to land. He asked me: 'I've heard a great deal,' said he, 'about … the St Kilda Mail.' Said he, 'I would like to get one of them myself.'

'Och,' said I, 'it's easy enough for you to get one.'

'Is it?' said he. 'I want to get it,' said he, 'complete. The float and the boat.'

And … 'Well,' said I, 'if you give me your address you will get…'

It was in London. That was where he lived. Said I, 'If you give me an address you will get it sent to you.'

'Will I?' said he.

'Oh, yes.'

'Well,' said he, 'I'll pay you.'

'Och,' said I, 'I don't know how much it will be,' said I, 'to go to London. And I don't know,' said I, 'if you will get it, … even if I throw it in the sea. You could,' said I, 'see to that when … you get it.'

Anyway, I had a brother … We went off and we made the float. Yes…

'What,' said he, 'do you want,' said he, 'for your trouble?'

I didn't know what to say to him. 'Och,' said I, 'a pound will do.'

He says, 'What? A pound!' said he. 'That wouldn't,' said he, 'pay for your trouble.'

'Och, it would,' said I. 'Och you could make it in two hours. You could make it in two hours, or three easy, only of course from beginning to end it would take more than ... two hours, what with putting it in the bark and things like that. But anyway, we made the float. A southwest gale came, fit to blow away the houses. The float was made and I ... took it down to the pier. I threw it in the sea and I didn't see it again. That was that and there wasn't a ship to be seen.

After a week or a fortnight a trawler came into the bay to shelter from the southwest wind. We went out to her. And he said: 'Who sent,' said he, 'the St Kilda Mail,' said he, 'who sent it off?'

Oh, they said that I had sent it.

'It only took,' said he, 'three days,' said he, 'to reach Shetland.'

Three days ... There was a bit in the paper about it.

The next summer a letter came from this old fellow ... from London, thanking me because he had got the float with the boat. It had been written on a ticket inside, inside the jar ... his address for it to be posted to. Now I never heard what he paid for it or anything but he said he had got it. He got it.[18]

Sheepskin floats, such as the one described above, were commonly made and used in the Hebrides until recent times. Here we see an early example of a traditional craft transformed to service the tourist industry!

The people of St Kilda whose recordings are held in the School of Scottish Studies Archives were very aware of their

18. Reprinted from *Tocher* 36–37, 446–450 (School of Scottish Studies, University of Edinburgh, 1981). Donald MacQueen recorded by John MacInnes (School of Scottish Studies Archives, SA1961.21). Transcription by Peggy McClements, translation by Cathie Scott.

heritage and the numerous texts and articles written about it. They were somewhat sceptical of the perceptions of those 'others' which purported knowledge of a people and a way of life that they may only have encountered in the course of a tourist visit of a few hours. This short presentation has served to introduce the language, culture and community life of St Kilda, much of which was shared with other people of the Hebrides. Through listening to their voices we can appreciate that the people of this island were active citizens rather than the passive ciphers represented in so much historiography.[19]

Figure 6. 'Hebrides' in Village Bay, 1938

Photo: Robert Atkinson (SSSA)

19.   Acknowledgements: Many thanks to Donald MacAulay, John MacInnes, Donald Meek, Caroline Milligan, Cathie Scott, Susan Pettigrew, Malcolm Brown, John Randall, Michael Robson, Domhnall Uilleam Stiùbhart, Alasdair MacEachen, Neil Ferguson, Mrs L MacDonald, Trish Campbell Botten, Morag MacLeod.

Naturalists and the 'St Kilda Library'

John A. Love

The archipelago of St Kilda boasts a biodiversity spectacle that is unmatched anywhere in the British Isles, and it even ranks high on a global scale. It is home to a million or more seabirds every summer, with the largest Northern Gannet colony in the world, and the largest puffin and Leach's petrel colonies in Britain. Until 1878 it was the only place in the UK where fulmars were to be found breeding. For such a small, treeless island St Kilda is ever accumulating an astonishing tally of migrant birds. Furthermore it has evolved its very own subspecies of wren and one (formerly two) subspecies of mice that are unique. For a thousand years or more it has been home to a breed of ancient sheep that is found nowhere else in the world. The geology and landforms are of great interest, being the only centre of Tertiary volcanic activity in the Outer Hebrides, one of a chain of 60 million year old volcanoes that so dominate the Inner Hebrides. St Kilda has the highest sheer cliff in Britain, the tallest sea stacks and many other dramatic coastal cliffs and caves. Its vegetation, especially on these cliff faces, is particularly noteworthy and, being an archipelago, it demonstrates many of the classic tenets of island biogeography (Love 2009).

In 1957 St Kilda came into the ownership of the National Trust for Scotland who quickly leased it to the Nature Conservancy when it became one of Britain's very first National Nature Reserves.

It was recognised as a Biosphere Reserve from 1976 (until 2000), and became a National Scenic Area in 1981. Three years later it was designated a Site of Special Scientific Interest and, in 1986, a World Heritage Site on account of its natural history. Under the European Directives it became a Special Protection Area in 1992 and then a Special Area for Conservation in 2005. St Kilda is reckoned to be one of the foremost dive locations in British waters, so when the fascinating marine life recently came to be extensively surveyed, this was added to the World Heritage listing in 2005 (when the cultural heritage finally and belatedly came to be recognised also). It remains the only dual World Heritage Site in Britain (for both natural and cultural importance), one of only 25 such out of nearly 1000 WHSs on the planet (Love 2009).

So, in this wonder-world of nature, it is strange that it was the St Kildan people, and their intriguing culture, that was invariably the main focus for visitors and dominated so many early accounts. Even those naturalists who did reach this far-flung outpost of the British Isles were easily distracted and it is not often recognised just how many of the classic and oft-quoted treatises on the St Kildans were actually penned by geologists, botanists and zoologists. In pursuit of their speciality interests these men – and they were largely men – often strived to stay longer to explore the islands more thoroughly and also to get to know the islanders better by tapping their intimate knowledge of the wildlife. This is a theme I develop in more detail in my recent book *A natural history of St Kilda* (2009). In a largely Gaelic community it was often the minister or schoolteacher who acted as go-between.

Seabirds and sheep were vital to the St Kildans' survival. The former were exploited by many island communities in the Hebrides but none depended upon them quite as much as the St Kildans. The latter, the unique Soay sheep, came to be replaced in the nineteenth century – as elsewhere in the Hebrides – by Blackfaces and it was only the inaccessibility of the island of Soay (from whence the breed derived its name) that saved them from extinction. The familiar flock that now roams Hirta for all to see were reintroduced there from Soay in 1932, after the blackfaces had been removed. Another isolated flock, perhaps more mixed and a less venerable lineage, survived on the island of Boreray and is now recognised as a rare breed in its own right (Harman 1997, Love 2009).

So who were these pioneering naturalists and scientists who ventured fifty miles out into the Atlantic to survey St Kilda's lonely shores? Although there are earlier brief references to St Kilda, its seabirds and sheep, the first – and some say the best – book about St Kilda was written by Martin Martin in 1697. This was a time when some further-flung outposts of the British Empire on the other side of the world were better known than the Hebrides – let alone St Kilda. So Martin, an educated gentleman from Skye with an eye on a medical career took it upon himself to put the matter right. What makes his account stand out is the fact that he was a Gaelic speaker so could communicate with the islanders directly. And this he did to full effect.

Martin learnt when the seabirds returned to their breeding colonies, when they laid their eggs and if they would lay again if the first egg was taken. Such intimate detail was vital for the islanders to exploit the seabird harvest effectively. Martin was able to deduce just how many auk eggs the islanders harvested each spring, though he did not relish them quite as did his hosts! Two or three visits for eggs could be made to guillemot ledges early in the season, but they dare not take a fulmar's egg since it would not relay. Most interesting of all, and unique in ornithological accounts, was his description of the now extinct great auk. Being flightless it was probably easy prey for the hungry islanders. Not surprisingly it was rare and little known by the eighteenth century and when four islanders caught one on Stac an Armin around 1840 they killed it because they thought it was a witch! It was the last one ever seen in Britain and within a few years the species was totally extinct.

Martin was not strictly a naturalist perhaps, but with his medical bent he sought to learn about herbal and other remedies, and collected all sorts of 'curiosities' such as rocks, minerals, shells, bird skins etc. He was also intensely interested in the supernatural and rituals, at a time when much of the remote Hebrides still preserved elements of paganism in their culture.

During the century following Martin visits by outsiders were few, although a succession of ministers, including Alexander Buchan and Kenneth MacAulay, left useful accounts with some natural history notes, mainly referring to the habits and harvesting of seabirds.

The first scientist to reach St Kilda was probably a mineralogist called Edward Daniel Clarke, later to become a professor in Cambridge. He was on St Kilda during July and August 1797 so got to know the islanders well but seems to have largely ignored the geology. Two years later Lord Brougham diverted to St Kilda, having failed to reach Iceland. In his party was Robert Campbell of Shawfield, Laird of Islay, who made a first collection of St Kilda's plants, a credible 53 species in all considering he also fell in love with a local girl during his visit.

It would be Guernsey-born John MacCulloch who made the first survey of St Kilda's rocks in 1815, the first visitor for over a year. The minister at that time was Lachlan Macleod from Skye. He was away when MacCulloch arrived but others had not been impressed by him.

In complete contrast the Reverend Neil MacKenzie stands out, not only by his efforts towards his flock and to the development of the community as a whole, but because he kept detailed notes on the wildlife. Curiously when this much-loved minister finally left St Kilda in 1844 he knew nothing about the demise of the last great auk. If it happened after he had left, and especially if a date of 1848 given for the incident by the folklorist Alexander Carmichael is correct, the St Kilda great auk would indeed have been the last of its kind anywhere on the planet (Love in prep).

Mackenzie relished company, and often shared his knowledge with naturalists on their perambulations, and doubtless gleaned from them in return. Only a year after his arrival in 1830, Mackenzie befriended a keen young naturalist George Clayton Atkinson, and his brother. During their four-day visit the minister showed them a peregrine eyrie from which two young islanders took two chicks for them, which they hoped to keep in captivity. Atkinson next persuaded two St Kildans to scale the 'inaccessible pinnacle' of Stac Biorach in exchange for some tobacco. He collected detailed bird notes (which included some notable errors – he mistakenly added great auk to his list for instance!) but his interesting account was not published in full until 2001.

Atkinson was to move in distinguished natural history circles which included the engraver Thomas Bewick, the eminent botanist William Hooker and an intrepid zoologist William MacGillivray. It is unfortunate that MacGillivray, a Gaelic speaker brought up in Harris who rose to be Professor of Natural History at Aberdeen University, never himself visited St Kilda. He would have known all about it however since most voyagers to the islands, including the Factor collecting rents, departed from Harris. It was left to his adventurous 18 year old son John to make one of the earliest natural history collections there, again tapping into the local knowledge of the islanders themselves and the 'worthy minister' Rev. Mackenzie of course. On their first excursion the pair found 50 plant species but in his four day stay he managed 'a very meagre account' of the insects, just 18 species. He was more successful with the bird life and gave a lengthy description of the seabird harvest.

Macgillivray went on to follow a fruitful career as naturalist on naval survey ships on the other side of the world, and for four years was drinking buddy of the surgeon Thomas Henry Huxley ('Darwin's Bulldog') aboard HMS *Rattlesnake*. A year after MacGillivray's visit the Paisley-born naturalist Rev. James Wilson arrived but could add little to Macgillivray's faunal list. He did undertake the National Census, totalling 96 people in 28 families, the older men 'we may call practised ornithologists, or cragsmen'. Wilson did go on to pen what some consider to be one of the best accounts of St Kilda and its inhabitants, but few other naturalists were to venture out until a more regular summer steamer service was instigated in the 1870s (Meek 2010).

The steamers – *Dunara Castle*, *Hebridean* and the *Hebrides* – made St Kilda more accessible but many naturalists stayed only the few hours that the cruises made available to them. One entomologist, Dr Norman Joy, did not even attempt the lengthy voyage himself but prevailed upon a willing passenger to rip up clumps of grass and haystacks for him, together with sheep's dung birds' nests for him to examine in the comfort of his own home! In 1875 one of the very first to take advantage of a steamer service was the advocate George Seton who, on the strength of a few hours ashore (and, admittingly, some painstaking and time-consuming research) went on to write one of the most detailed histories of St Kilda, still well regarded to this day. In contrast, around that same time, an uncompromising Edinburgh lawyer and journalist John Sands spent many months on St Kilda, befriended the islanders, fell out with the minister Rev. John MacKay and strived to better the lot of the St Kildans. Although neither were naturalists the accounts of Seton and Sands rank as some of the most informed and informative in the St Kilda library.

Several distinguished men of science were able to reach St Kilda under their own steam. In 1884 Alexander Ross, the noted Inverness architect, accompanied the sportsman and ornithologist Henry Evans aboard his yacht *Erne*. Ross managed to improve on MacCulloch's geological survey and then provided

Professor John Wesley Judd of Imperial College, London with all his rock samples. Judd went on to write a short paper on St Kilda's geology – without ever having been there! Henry Evans, on the other hand, became a regular visitor to the archipelago in his yacht. Ten years later Professor Sir Archibald Geikie, Director General of the Geological Survey, chartered a boat from Lewis to undertake his own definitive studies of St Kilda's rocks.

Another regular visitor was the illustrious Stirlingshire naturalist J A Harvie-Brown in his yacht *Shiantelle*. His last visit was in 1896 but aboard the Irish cutter *Granuaile* in the company of the Irish botanists Robert Lloyd Praeger and Richard Manliffe Barrington. They were intent on visiting Rockall but failing to land they turned their attention to St Kilda instead. In 1883 Barrington, in the company of some St Kildan cragsmen, had become the first outsider to scale the impenetrable Stac Biorach and, unable to bring back a specimen of the St Kilda wren for critical examination, he went on to extend the islands' plant list. It would be another two years before the London ornithologist Charles Dixon procured the first wren skin, finally to prove its uniqueness.

W Eagle Clarke from the Royal Scottish Museum paid several visits to St Kilda, some of them aboard the Duchess of Bedford's yacht *Sapphire,* and finally solved the wren problem in 1915. He did not merit it being called a separate species, merely a subspecies and went on to resolve a similar issue over the St Kilda mice, according them sub-specific status also.

In 1905 the entomologist Rev. James Waterston from the British Museum (whose son Rodger also became an eminent zoologist in the Royal Scottish Museum) had taken an interest in the mice and employed local St Kildan lads to catch them for him. John Sands made the interesting comment how the men of St Kilda were careful not to transport mice to Boreray and how they once demolished seven cleits to catch and kill one that escaped from their baggage! This must surely be one of the first recorded instances of bio-security on islands.

The demand for biological specimens (especially fulmars, Leach's petrels and St Kilda wrens) was to prove a lucrative sideline for the St Kildans and contributed in no small way to the development of a cash economy, which in turn reduced the islanders' independence leading to abandonment of their ancient way of life and ultimate evacuation. The Inverness architect Alexander Ross wrote:

> *The people have learned the value of money, and to enjoy many of the luxuries of civilised life ... Indeed they run a great risk of being spoiled by visitors who go there in considerable numbers annually.*

The islanders sold tweed, woollens, postcards and other souvenirs to day-tourists, and would often pose for photographs or give spinning and rock climbing demonstrations in exchange for money (Maclean 1972, Love 2006). This had not been the case however for long-stay visitors such as Norman Heathcote and his sister Evelyn in 1898–99, or for the wildlife photographers Richard and Cherry Kearton in 1896 and Oliver Pike in 1908 and 1910. The long-term friendships which these courteous visitors made on the island helped them record for posterity on both paper and film of a way of life that was soon to disappear forever.

Strangely, although it was Martin Martin who first attempted to map St Kilda, it was not until 1927 that this was achieved to modern standards. A retired Ordnance Surveyor John Mathieson undertook this daunting task in the company of a 25 year old geologist Alexander Cockburn and a 19 year old botanist John Gladstone (Quine 1988 etc). Their work was definitive, precise and thorough. Mathieson's map remains the standard while Cockburn took many photographs of the islanders that were to become classics. St Kilda was evacuated only three years later.

Several homesick islanders chose to return by steamer every summer where they continued to live off the land and seabirds; they also received payment for ferrying steamer passengers ashore for the day, and by selling their wares – including bird skins and eggs. In 1931 a group of graduate students from Oxford and Cambridge arrived to study natural history and recorded the last of the St Kilda house mice. The ornithologist David Lack also collected insects while the botanist Charles Petch struggled to add much new to John Gladstone's plant lists. The party did not integrate easily with the islanders, in complete contrast to another visiting naturalist Robert Atkinson in 1938 (Love 2007). His intimate portraits of old Finlay MacQueen, Mrs Gillies and her son Neil adorn the pages of Atkinson's wonderful book *Island Going* – still a cult read for anyone interested in remote islands. Atkinson confirmed the extinction of the house mice and was amazed to have travelled to St Kilda aboard the same *Dunara Castle* that had transported his heroes, the Keartons, in 1896 and, indeed, had made its first visit to St Kilda in 1877! It was not finally broken up until 1948 (Meek 2010).

So many names crop up repeatedly in St Kilda's poignant human story but it is only when one looks closer at their own background that one realises just how many contributions to the St Kilda library were in fact made by naturalists. Although the islanders are now gone, St Kilda remains the same spectacular group of islands with a natural heritage that is unsurpassed by any other of the British Isles. And future generations of naturalists still have a lot to discover.

References

Atkinson, R. 1949 *Island Going* London (Reprint, 1995 Birlinn, Edinburgh)

Barrington, R.M. 1913 'Ascent of Stack na Biorrach, St Kilda' *Alpine Journal* 27, 195–202

Brougham, Lord 1871 *Memoirs of the Life and Times of Lord Brougham written by himself* London and Edinburgh

Buchan, A. 1727 *A Description of St Kilda* Lumisden and Robertson, Edinburgh (reprinted with substantial alterations by Miss Buchan, 1752.)

Clarke Edward Daniel 1824 *The Life and Remains of Edward Daniel Clarke* Ed W Otter, London

Clarke, W.E. 1914 'Notes on mice of St Kilda' *Scottish Naturalist* 124–128

Clarke, W.E 1915 'Wren, its status, plumages and habits' *Scottish Naturalist* 291–296

Cockburn, A.M. 1934 'The Geology of St Kilda' *Transactions of the Royal Society of Edinburgh* 35 part 2 no.21, 511–54

Dixon, C. 1885 'The Ornithology of St Kilda' *Ibis* 5 (3), 69–97, 358–362

Geikie, Sir A. 1897 *The Ancient Volcanoes of Britain* London, 2, 405–417

Gladstone, J. 1928 'Notes on the flora' In St Kilda (ed. J. Mathieson). *Scottish Geographical Magazine* 44(2): 77–79

Harman, M. 1996 *An Isle called Hirte* Maclean Press, Isle of Skye

Harvie-Brown, J.A. and Buckley, T.E. 1888 *A Vertebrate Fauna of the Outer Hebrides* Edinburgh

Heathcote, N. 1900 *St Kilda* London

Joy, N.H. 1908 'Notes on Coleoptera from St Kilda, mainly collected from birds' nests' *Annals of Scottish Natural History* 33–35

Kearton, R. 1897 *With Nature and a Camera* London (Reprint Melven Press, Inverness 1978)

Lack D. 1931 Diary Oxford University Library

Love J.A. 2005b Seabird Resources and Fowling in Scotland. In Randall, J. (ed) *Traditions of Sea-bird Fowling in the North Atlantic Region*. Islands Book Trust, Stornoway

Love J.A. 2007 Natural History and the St Kilda Library In *St Kilda: myth and reality* 32 pp Ed John Randall, Islands Book Trust, Port of Ness.

Love J A (2008) *Three centuries of Highland Naturalists* Island Notes, Islands Book Trust, Stornoway

Love J.A. (2009) *A natural history of St Kilda*. Birlinn, Edinburgh

Macaulay, K. 1764 *The History of St Kilda* London

MacCulloch, J. 1819 *A Description of the Western Isles of Scotland* 2 and map 3, 75, Hurst, Robinson and Co., London

Macgillivray, J. 1842 'An account of the island of St. Kilda, chiefly with reference to its natural history; from notes made during a visit in July 1840' *Edinburgh New Philosophical Journal* 32, 47–178

MacKenzie, J.B. 1905 'Antiquities and old customs in St Kilda, compiled from notes made by Rev. Neil MacKenzie, minister of St Kilda, 1829–43', *Proceedings of the Society of Antiquaries of Scotland* 39 (1904–5), 397–402

MacKenzie, J.B. 1911 *Episode in the Life of the Rev. Neil MacKenzie at St Kilda from 1829 to 1843* (privately publ.)

MacKenzie, N. 1905 'Notes on the birds of St Kilda' *Annals of Scottish Natural History* 14, 75–80, 141–153

MacLean, C. 1972 *Island on the Edge of the World: The Story of St Kilda*. Tom Stacey Ltd. (Revised edition Cannongate, Edinburgh 1996)

Martin, M. 1698 *A Late Voyage to St Kilda* London (Reprint 1986 James Thin, The Mercat Press Edinburgh)

Mathieson, J. 1928 'St Kilda', *Scottish Geographical Magazine* 44, 65–90

Mathieson, J. and Cockburn, A.M. 1929 'St Kilda' *Transactions of the Edinburgh Geological Society* 12 1929, 287–288

Meek, D.E. 2010 *Steamships to St Kilda*. Islands Book Trust, Isle of Lewis

Petch, C.P. 1933 'The vegetation of St. Kilda.' *Journal of Ecology* 21, 92–100

Pike, O.G. 1910 *Through Birdland Byways with Pen and Camera* London

Pike, O.G. 1946 *Nature and My Cine Camera* London

Praeger, R.L. 1897 'Flora of St. Kilda' (note) *Annals of Scottish Natural History* 1897, 53

Quine, D.A. 1988 *St Kilda Portraits* Downland Press, Frome

Quine, D.A. (ed.) 2001 *Expeditions to the Hebrides By George Clayton Atkinson in 1831 and 1833* Maclean Press, Isle of Skye

Ross, A. 1884 'A visit to the island of St Kilda', *Transactions of the Inverness Scientific Society and Field Club* 3 (1883–8), 72–91

Sands, J. 1878 *Out of the World; or, Life in St Kilda* Edinburgh

Seton, G. 1878 *St Kilda Past and Present* Edinburgh (1980 reprint, James Thin, The Mercat Press, Edinburgh)

Waterson, J. 1905 'Notes on the mice and birds of St Kilda' *Annals of Scottish Natural History* 14, 199–202

Wilson, J. 1842 *A Voyage round the Coasts of Scotland and the Isles* 2, Edinburgh

Wilson, J. 1842 'Additional Notice Regarding St Kilda' *Edinburgh New Philosophical Journal* 32, 178–180

The Natural History of St Kilda

Richard Luxmoore

St Kilda's natural history, like most aspects of this fascinating archipelago, has attracted a considerable amount of attention in the copious published literature. It has been expertly summarised by John Love in *A natural history of St Kilda* and it would be pointless to try to add to or improve on this excellent book. Most of the early references are largely anecdotal and it was not until the mid twentieth century that serious specialist studies were carried out and published. These give us most of our factual and quantitative information about the subject but the early studies shed light on three important areas: the former presence of now-extinct species (notably the Great Auk and the St Kilda House Mouse), the human use of the seabirds and other natural resources, and some indication of changes in abundance of a few species. The latter is only possible at a coarse scale because the estimates of population size were seldom made using methods that would be considered necessary for such comparisons today. The human use of seabirds is interesting not only because it was the cornerstone of human survival on the islands but also because it helps to show how seabirds can be sustainably harvested – an extremely tricky task with such long-lived and slow-maturing species.

Scientific studies have been carried out since the 1930s and are particularly concentrated on the sheep and the seabirds. The sheep have been subject to one of the longest running studies of a large mammal anywhere in the world and have resulted in two monographs (*Island Survivors – The ecology of the Soay sheep of St Kilda* by P.A. Jewell, C. Milner and J.M. Boyd; and *Soay Sheep – dynamics and selection in an island population* by T. Clutton Brock and J. Pemberton). A concise summary of the bird life can be found in *Birds of St Kilda* by S. Murray but there is as yet no monograph on the seabirds, though they have been the subject of many published scientific papers. Seabirds are very much part of the marine ecosystem, deriving almost all of their food from the sea and visiting the islands for only a short part of the year to breed. They are an indication of the extraordinary richness of the seas around St Kilda which far surpasses the terrestrial environment.

In reality, St Kilda sits at the eastern extremity of the Atlantic Ocean and commands a priviledged position at the edge of one of the world's greatest ocean currents, the North Atlantic Drift. This gives it a unique position to benefit from the nutrients that the current brings and to play host to the great diversity of marine life attracted to it or being carried along by it. Although St Kilda ranks as one of the foremost dive destinations in Europe it is an aspiration that is seldom realised by amateur divers because of the difficulty and expense of access. Similar difficulties face scientific investigation of the sea and, as a result, relatively little has been written on St Kilda's marine life. Following the declaration of surrounding seas as part of the World Heritage Site, one of very few marine sites around the world, the years to come may bring great advances in scientific study, effective conservation and in literature on this most important aspect of St Kilda's natural history.

The Historiography of
the Archaeology of St Kilda

Susan Bain

In order to discuss the historiography of archaeology I believe it is useful to define these terms. This may seem a basic question but in the context of a conference and publication looking at assumptions and challenging perceived wisdom then it's good to clarify: historiography is the study of the history and methodology of the discipline of history. Archaeology is the study of past human societies, through the recovery of their material culture and environmental data which they have left behind. Archaeologists look at artefacts, buildings, architecture and biofacts/ecofacts (these are things not changed by people but left behind by their activities e.g. seeds, human bone). Archaeology has been likened to a crime scene and the subsequent forensic activity and this is a useful analogy; from the evidence left behind archaeologists try to recreate the most likely event that led to that. From the analysis of this information we hope to learn more about the past.

Human history spans approximately 2.5 million years. For 99% of that time human society was pre-historic, which means there are no written records. So therefore the only way to begin to understand how many past societies worked is to study archaeology. Archaeology is also important in the understanding of the historic period; history itself – the written record – is a cultural artefact, so even within the historic period archaeology is essential to understanding past societies. History can be re-written by archaeology and archaeology can be informed by history. On St Kilda where the written record describes such a short period of its settlement and is dominated by views from the outside then archaeology may be of even greater importance.

The exact origins of archaeology as a discipline are uncertain, but the origins of modern archaeology in Europe emerge during the Enlightenment in the 17th and 18th centuries. By understanding the history of archaeology and how it has been influenced we can more critically analyse archaeological writings in general and St Kilda specifically. The early antiquarians in the 16th and 17th centuries tended to be ministers and vicars and they described, surveyed and drew the monuments they encountered in their parishes and interpreted them as best they could, given that they had no means of knowing their age or usage.

By the late 1700s some were attempting a more methodical approach. Thomas Jefferson (more famous for being a US President than an archaeologist) explored an Indian burial mound on his estate in 1784 and crucially avoided the practice of just digging down but cut a wedge out of the mound so that he could look at the layers and draw conclusions. He described what he saw:

> *Appearances certainly indicate that it has derived both origin and growth from the accustomary collection of bones, and deposition of them together; that the first collection had been deposited on the common surface of the earth, a few stones put over it, and then a covering of earth, that the second had been laid on this ... and so on ... (Notes on the State of Virginia: 224)*

What Jefferson proposed was that the mound had been in use for a long time with a sequence of burials, not built after a single event, like a battle. He supported this position with evidence drawn from observation.

Throughout the 1800s there was a development of archaeology as an academic discipline – based on methodology and an understanding of strata. A three age system – the Stone Age, Bronze Age and Iron Age – had been proposed and adopted in the 1820s and so now artefacts and sites could be dated relative to one another. Typologies of monument and artefact meant that similar things could be compared and contrasted and sequences developed. Throughout the 20th century archaeology has continued to develop with the technology and science of the time and huge strides have been made with the development of scientific dating techniques such as radio carbon dating; and other techniques, such as isotope analysis and DNA sequencing, have enabled archaeologists to identify origins of artefacts and even ethnicity. However, amongst all this science we have to remember that archaeologists are people and there is certainly debate within the archaeological community as to what extent the archaeologist interprets the archaeology – Schiffer (1987) noted that '*the behaviour of the archaeologist is the greatest source of variability in the archaeological record*'. We bring our culture, class, ethnicity, politics and gender to the table and that must be recognised.

If we return to the Indian Burial mounds from the US, the history of their interpretation illustrates how preconceptions can colour archaeological interpretations. Burial mounds were constructed from about 3000 BC to the 16th century by various indigenous cultures across the eastern and southern US – and attracted the attention of the earliest antiquarians and archaeologists.

Although Jefferson concluded that these were Native American sites when he excavated in the 1780s, ten years later others were attributing them to the Vikings. By the mid 1800s many held the opinion that the mounds were not Native American but had been constructed by Greeks, Europeans, Africans, the lost Tribes of Israel, inhabitants of Atlantis, anyone in fact other than ancestors of the people living there now.

The evidence hadn't changed, it was still the same bones and the same artefacts but what had changed were the ideas of the time. Many were now happy to believe that the Native Americans were too simple to have constructed the mounds and the artefacts found within them. If the mound builders were European then the land grab of Indian land was justified as taking back what had once been European. It is much easier to conquer a people if you believe they have no legitimacy to the land and are culturally inferior.

Throughout the later 19th and early 20th centuries a belief in European superiority not only fuelled colonialism but also influenced the interpretation of many archaeological sites across the globe; with many sites being attributed to outside influences rather than indigenous cultures. Today even though archaeology is increasingly science based, site interpretation is still influenced by prevailing thought and culture.

So how has the archaeological evidence on St Kilda been portrayed, and does it tell us about the St Kildans or the archaeologist? Martin Martin gives us the first written account of the antiquities of St Kilda after his visit in 1694; he doesn't excavate but notes antiquities and attempts to explain older buildings. He describes the layout and method of construction of the Amazon's House in Gleann Mor, noting that it '*is built of stone, without any wood, lime, earth or mortar to cement it and is in the form of a circle*'. Martin Martin also refers to the associated myth of the warrior Queen, stating that it is 'in their tradition'. He clearly does not believe the building was constructed by a mythical figure, but together with a physical description of the building also describes local folklore. Also he comments on a similar building on Borerary, noting that is of a similar construct but larger and that by tradition it was built by a hermit. What we do have in Martin's account is an attempt to describe rationally what he was seeing, to take a step back from his own culture and describe it to an outside audience. Martin would have been well versed in the philosophy of the time – the late 17th century is the Age of Reason, with the development of both rationalism and empiricism and the detachment of philosophy from theology. What we have in Martin's account is an attempt to use observation and reason to explain the unknown; this is a very different way of thinking from the medieval period. His visit to St Kilda was under the patronage of the secretary of the Royal Society, Hans Sloane, antiquarian, natural historian and collector and so Martin was writing his account to gain acceptance and standing with an urban, educated and distant audience.

It is not until the 19th century that we see a more fully developed antiquarian approach to the antiquities of St Kilda. The Rev. Neil MacKenzie, minister on St Kilda, became an inadvertent archaeologist when he uncovered the *cnocan sithichean* – fairy mounds – whilst clearing and draining the arable land in Village Bay in the 1830s. He notes their contents: pottery and bone, and differences in construction. He gives a detailed enough description that later archaeologists are confident in categorising these as pre-historic burial mounds. Although MacKenzie uses the term fairy mound, I believe it is fair to assume that he did not attribute these to the work of fairies even though such beliefs were still widespread in Highland Scotland at the time. This was a term in common usage, one that anyone would know to what he was referring and he does so in a private journal not an academic essay. MacKenzie is certainly aware of antiquarianism and its interests when in the course of building an enclosure dyke he sets large stones that '*were lying flat and occupying a good deal of space I raised them up on end. They may puzzle some future antiquary*' (MacKenzie 1911).

MacKenzie is not an antiquarian but would have certainly been aware of a growing interest in antiquities in Scottish society – the Society of Antiquaries of Scotland was founded in 1783 and began publishing in the 1790s. He must have been aware of the First Statistical Account of Scotland in the 1790s which was completed by ministers and in which many archaeological monuments are described. Mackenzie's approach does not seem to be overly skewed by his religion or status as minister. He describes what he finds but offers little comment – as a well educated man he is perhaps aware of the necessity of clear description and also of the limits of his knowledge.

In 1870 Capt. Thomas, the naval surveyor, published a paper in the Proceedings of the Society of Antiquaries of Scotland (of which he was a member) '*On the primitive dwellings and hypogea of the Outer Hebrides*' – in it he tries to draw parallels between sites and compares similar structures across the islands. He compares the souterrains of the Western Isles and further afield, and the cleits, with structures in Shetland and the Faeroes and attempts to date them on the knowledge he has. As a surveyor and photographer his strength is in the measured site plans of two structures in Gleann Mor and also of the internal fittings of a contemporary blackhouse. Again we see a belief that if things are measured and compared then knowledge will come from that – that a reasoned and structured approach will result in understanding. The Victorian Age was one of invention and possibility; scientific knowledge was increasing rapidly with advances in every field – medicine, engineering, biology and so on. Knowledge and understanding of the world was developing at a rapid rate and Thomas's work reflects this. He was a surveyor – mapping the world so it can be known and understood. He was also a member of the Society of Antiquaries and of an Edinburgh Photographic Club, when photography was in its infancy and he is part of this exciting new world. In his paper Thomas starts from contemporary structures and attempts to work back. It is interesting that he views modern structures as archaeology, and this approach to St Kilda (and perhaps the whole of Western Scotland), where there is little distinction between the contemporary population of St Kilda and the past, is a common theme of the later Victorian accounts.

The first 'excavation' that we have an account of is by John Sands in 1876,when he carried out an excavation of the souterrain, and elsewhere, and correctly identified some of the stones he found as stone tools. It was again excavated by Kearton in 1896 and Mathieson in 1927, although none of these three were archaeologists but rather just interested parties who had the time and inclination. Archaeology as a pure discipline was not pursued on St Kilda until the latter half of the 20th century and until then archaeological information had to be teased out from the anthropology, folklore, politics and social observation.

In the later 20th century there is a sustained programme of archaeological survey, excavation and publication. The process of archaeological survey and excavation is subject to a series of decisions and each one may reflect either an individual or cultural bias: where to survey, what method to use, where to excavate, what to record, what to keep and what to throw away are all small decisions that impact on the interpretation. These decisions can be influenced by the background and experience of the archaeologist and team, funding availability, time constraints or research agendas. On St Kilda accessibility of sites is a major factor in what has and has not been looked at. It should come as no surprise that archaeological excavation has concentrated in the Village Bay area, close to facilities and services although it must also be recognised that the densest concentration of upstanding remains are here too.

The University of Durham undertook a series of excavations in the 1980s looking at the mid 19th century remains in Village

Bay. This was part of a research strategy developed between the Trust and the University of Durham's archaeology department. The strategy was to begin with the recent remains and work back in time – a strategy Thomas had adopted in the 1870s. This work resulted in the confirmation of Blackhouse W as a kiln barn and also looked at House 6 (prior to its refurbishment) and House 8 which had a blackhouse underlying it. The resulting publication by Norman Emery (*Excavations on St Kilda*) details many of the 19th and 20th century artefacts as well as earlier material unearthed. These excavations concentrated on a time during which the majority of the documentary material was composed. To some extent the archaeological evidence supports and compliments the historical documents; the large amount of imported goods indicating increasing contact with mainland markets. This contact and availability of a range of imported goods, found in every midden, is perhaps downplayed in the historical record, which tends to emphasise the inaccessibility and lack of regular contact between St Kilda and the mainland.

The excavation of 19th and 20th century sites, inhabited within living memory, was a significant development of archaeology in the later 20th century. Prior to this most archaeologists would not have recorded this material in any detail. Throughout the 1990s and into the 21st century excavations were carried out by the University of Glasgow and later Glasgow University Archaeological Research Division (GUARD) at various locations around the Village Bay area: on Mullach Sgar and in An Lag, and in the Village. At the same time research was being carried out by Professor Andrew Fleming from the University of Lampeter on the landscape and stone tools, and Professor Andy Meharg of Aberdeen University who was carrying out research into the soils. The results of Glasgow's work are due to be published soon (Harden & Lelong 2011).

In summary, the archaeological evidence for the past 4,000 years tells us that St Kilda was linked culturally to the Western

Isles and mainland Scotland. We know this because we can see clear parallels in building styles and artefacts. The souterrain is clearly identifiable as such and can be readily compared in size, shape and construction with those in Skye, the Western Isles and indeed the Atlantic coasts of Ireland & Cornwall. Pottery recovered from Mullach Sgar is similar to that found within the Iron Age deposits from Sollas in North Uist and also sites in South Uist. Some of the structures in Gleann Mor have parallels in the Western and Northern Isles dating to the mid to late 1st millennium AD. All this is sound evidence that Hirta's communities travelled to other islands or received voyagers from other places, or both; that they saw or heard about trends in architecture and chose to reproduce them.

There are still many areas where the archaeological record perhaps raises more questions than answers. The so-called hidey-holes in the scree slopes of Mullach Sgar are still an enigma. Three of them were excavated in the 1990s. Stone tools were recovered, but not from the floor deposits or from within the buildings – so they could represent later use of the area, rather than the use of the structures. The range of stone tools recovered, including a stone bar or hoe blade, a saddle quern and a rubber, would normally suggest an Iron Age date. However on St Kilda where there is no evidence for a distinction between Iron Age, medieval or post-medieval stone tools this date range can be extended. Unfortunately no other dating evidence was found, other than no artefacts from the 19th or 20th centuries. So from the archaeological evidence we cannot determine their use nor the period of construction, other than pre-19th century.

Their use can be conjectured by looking at what is going on in the immediate area and by looking at other similar sites. It may be that they were associated with the use of the scree as a stone tool quarry site – an Iron Age tea-hut!; or have a link with the early Christian settlement (monastic cells or even a funerary function); or they may be hidey-holes, built to hide from the Barbary pirates who raided the west coast of Britain, the Faeroes and Iceland in the 17th century. They could of course be a combination of these – the function of any building or feature can change. Houses become cattle byres, scree shelters become hidey-holes and so on. In the absence of any datable evidence from them, then we can only propose a best fit theory. The theories proposed do reflect the archaeologist as much as the archaeological evidence. I favour the hidey-holes theory, but this may be because I have visited similar sites in the Faeroe Islands and was struck not just by the similarity of the site but by the island group and culture. Where there are clear similarities in one area we must be careful not to apply them universally. Just because St Kilda has a similar dramatic landscape to the Faroe Islands and their populations share a similar resource base of seabirds and subsistence agriculture does not mean that they respond in the same way architecturally. There is a suggestion that St Kilda was raided in the 17th century but no evidence from the scree structures that they belong to this date. However with the news dominated by Somali pirate raids and popular western culture embracing pirate films (Pirates of the Caribbean – Dead Man's Chest grossed over $1 billion), then I would suggest a pirate theory is understandable in this context.

Similarly, the 'boat-shaped' settings in An Lag are an archaeological feature that has undergone a change in interpretation over the years (note the use of inverted commas in 'boat-shaped'). These stone settings had been mapped and identified by the Ordnance Survey in the 1960s and excavated by a team from Dundee University in the 1970s. Boat-shaped settings are associated elsewhere in Scotland with Norse burials; however the excavation in the 1970s was inconclusive with neither human remains nor artefacts being recovered and with a Bronze Age radio carbon date from a peat deposit. The absence of human remains from a burial site is not that odd, the soil conditions may not be conducive to preservation, but a burial from either the Bronze of Viking periods may be expected to contain grave goods which would have survived.

In the 1990s it was decided to look at these features again to resolve the date and function. However, the same problem of lack of any artefacts or human remains, or dating evidence led to a very similar debate to 20 years previously – that it was inconclusive. More recently the shape, size and landscape setting of these features has been re-assessed. In size and plan they are very similar to the cleits in An Lag, and so the pragmatic conclusion reached is that some are robbed out cleits and others peat stack stances, known from elsewhere in the Western Isles, for example Mingulay. So now the best-fit theory is that they are neither Bronze Age burials, nor Viking graves but demolished cleits.

In summary, each piece of archaeological work that has been carried out over the past 20 years has added to the greater picture. With technological developments we can benefit from non invasive techniques. Resistivity and magnetometry surveys now produce results, even in the difficult geological conditions of Village Bay. Investigations of pollen & biogeochemistry in the soils of Hirta have illuminated changes in vegetation and land use over the last several thousand years. Archaeological information, although science based, is about interpretation and we have to be mindful of that when reading an archaeological text. From the dry data, stories are created about the past and we interpret the past in a way that makes sense to us.

Today we are in a position where we have St Kilda on a see-saw, we want to draw it back into the fold of the Western Isles, portray it as not so remote and isolated, but at the same time we are enthralled by the exoticism and romanticism of the *Island at the Edge of the World* and perhaps want to keep it that way. Perhaps the reality is that it is both. It is quite clearly very much part of the Western Isles and the archaeological evidence shows strong links with the other islands in the Western Isles – the building style, stone tools and the pottery shapes. But there are oddities too – the cleits in their vast number is an obvious case in point and the number of artefacts associated with seabirds is unusual. The archaeological evidence supports the view that there are more similarities than differences, and we should do well to heed Martin Martin who noted that '*it is weakness and folly to value things merely on account of their distance*'.

References

Christenson, A.L. (Ed.) (1989) *Tracing Archaeology's Past: The Historiography of Archaeology*

Fleming, A. (2005) *St Kilda and the Wider World: Tales of an Iconic Island*

Harden, J. & Lelong, O. (2011) *St Kilda Archaeological Monograph*

Jefferson, T. (1782) *Notes on the State of Virginia* Electronic Text Center, University of Virginia Library

MacKenzie, J.B. (Ed.) (1911) *Episode in the Life of the Rev. Neil MacKenzie at St Kilda*

Martin Martin (1698) *A Voyage to St Kilda*

Schiffer, M. (1987) *Current Anthropology* 28

Thomas, F.L.W. (1870) *On the Primitive Dwellings and Hypogea of the Outer Hebrides* in Proceedings of the Society Antiquaries of Scotland

Wikipedia *History of Archaeology*

'Eileanaich Cian a' Chuain' / 'The Remote Islanders of the Sea'? Towards a Re-examination of the Role of Church and Faith in St Kilda

Donald E. Meek

The role of church and faith in St Kilda is, perhaps, one of the most difficult themes that a conference speaker can be asked to tackle. The difficulties lie in two main areas. The first is that the centrality of the church (especially in its post-1820 form) to the life of that tiny community has guaranteed that it has been over-exposed in most of the literature. The second is that, until the publication of Michael Robson's landmark volume, the material for a properly detailed study of this subject, coupled with a balanced analytical narrative, had not been available.[1] To date, opinions have been formed largely through 'popular' accounts, rather than the thoroughly-researched ethnologically-based studies which both church and community merit. This is part of a general 'problem' with the continuous 'memorialising' of St Kilda. Out of the tsunami of 700-plus books and articles which has all but overwhelmed

---

1. Robson, *St Kilda: Church, Visitors and 'Natives'*.

the archipelago,[2] less than (perhaps) ten books can be justly regarded as properly authoritative, in the sense that they are founded firmly on a detailed examination of the St Kilda islands, coupled with residency and overall familiarity, as well as an exhaustive interaction with relevant sources, oral and literary, Gaelic and English. Exemplary works (large and small!) by Dr Mary Harman, Bill Lawson, Michael Robson and David Quine stand out as being the best by far among the putative ten.[3]

Books in Gaelic about St Kilda are exceptionally rare – only one springs to mind, written by Calum Ferguson of Point, Lewis.[4] Even books in English by native islanders are rare; the recent publication in 2010 of two books written in English by St Kildans was a landmark event.[5] These supplement the excellent, sensitive and unassuming publications of David Quine, who has given a particular place to the views and narratives of St Kildans themselves, and has put these residual St Kildans at the centre of their own world. Their narratives are invaluable in offering much-needed correctives to the 'popular' general works, not least in the area of religious experience, which is the concern of this paper.

'Popular' works (in English) on St Kilda, produced by a horde of visitors, tourists, journalists chasing 'good stories', 'my journey' narrators, undergraduates pursuing dissertations, theory-driven anthropologists and so on, have a long history, and are likely to remain the principal access route for many readers. Their

---

2. This estimate by John Randall is based on the Scottish Executive's listing of writings about St Kilda in its 2003 submission for enhanced World Heritage Site status.

3. Harman, *An Isle Called Hirte*; Lawson, *St Kilda and its Church*; Robson, *St Kilda: Church, Visitors and 'Natives'*; Quine, *St Kilda Portraits*.

4. MacFhearghuis, *Hiort: Far na laigh a' ghrian*.

5. Gillies, *The Truth about St Kilda*; MacDonald, *From Cleits to Castles*.

post-1960 ranks include the writings of Tom Steel[6] and Charles MacLean[7], now among the veterans of 'popular historiography' as applied to St Kilda. Steel's book, first produced in 1965 as a consequence of a Cambridge dissertation, and published initially by the National Trust for Scotland, remains, in its expanded and revised version, the most authoritative of the popular works, and is the first port of call for many on their literary voyage to St Kilda, its former inhabitants and its stacs.[8]

Silence and supremacy

Although MacLean and Steel did consult native St Kildans (e.g. Neil Ferguson, Neil Gillies and Lachie MacDonald) for their editions of 1972 and 1975 respectively, we have to recognise a third major problem in the existing literature: namely, the relative 'silence' of the St Kildan 'voice', which is conspicuous by its absence from existing 'popular' accounts, and has been allowed to surface clearly only since 1980 or so. The evidence left by the islanders themselves (and by those who lived in St Kilda for a prolonged period) requires to be taken into consideration in any assessment of the people's traditions and conventions, including (especially) those pertaining to church and faith.[9]

---

6. Steel, *The Life and Death of St Kilda*.

7. MacLean, *Island on the Edge of the World: Utopian St Kilda and its Passing*.

8. The publication of Steel's and MacLean's volumes in the period 1965–75 is fascinating, and one must wonder why they were produced at this time. Presumably they were, to some extent, 'evacuation anniversary markers' (commemorating 30, 40 and 45 years since St Kilda was evacuated). It is also possible that they are, to some extent incidentally, a response to the decolonisation of African countries in the 1960s.

9. Although Gaelic was the native language of the St Kildans, no books or articles about St Kilda written in Gaelic by the St Kildans themselves actually exist. The existing 'St Kildan voice' speaks and writes in English. Many reasons can be offered for this apparent

Much of the source material which has been used hitherto has been derived very largely from the impressions of nineteenth-century 'radicals', hacks and axe-grinders who aired their thoughts in English-language newspapers and books, most notably and formatively John Sands, who first arrived in St Kilda in 1875. The material is coloured to a large extent by the idiosyncrasies, preconceptions and aims of the writers, as Sands' work demonstrates. Sands' literary efforts, which established this distinctive genre, succeeded in achieving both good and bad for St Kilda. At one level, his book (in two different editions, 1876 and 1878) is a fascinating and well-written account of many aspects of St Kildan life, in which he expresses considerable admiration for the people and their conventions, with particularly graphic descriptions of their skills in fowling and cragsmanship. At another level, it is a reflection of Sands' own preoccupations, preconceptions, misconceptions and overall ambitions, especially in his crusade for social justice for the St Kildans. While championing their allegedly downtrodden condition, Sands created controversy, and in the process he blackened the character of those with whom he disagreed.[10]

---

contradiction, which was discussed at the 80th Anniversary St Kilda Conference in August 2010. Among these are: (a) St Kildans' lack of confidence in writing or presenting themselves in Gaelic; (b) the early establishment of English as the principal language of discourse relating to St Kilda, largely because of dominant external interest; and (c) the desire of St Kildan writers such as Gillies and MacDonald to have their 'voices' heard within an ongoing discussion/debate which was/is being conducted in English. In this respect, the literature of St Kilda offers a sharp contrast to the literary output of the Blasket Islands, Co. Kerry, Ireland, which is in Irish.

10. For this paper, I was unable to consult Sands' 1876 edition. A thorough comparative study of both 1876 and 1878 editions might reveal more about Sands' motives and changing perceptions of his own role and that of the Rev. John MacKay.

The personalised and politically partisan dimension of Sands' work has not been given the weight it deserves, especially in the discussion of the Rev. John MacKay, the unfortunate Free Church minister of St Kilda (1865–89), whose incumbency is still judged largely in the light of Sands' evidence, which remains an enormous obstacle to any fair-minded assessment of church and faith in St Kilda.[11] While we may agree wholly with Emily MacLeod of MacLeod that MacKay was indeed 'narrow-minded perhaps',[12] we should be very wary of accepting all that Sands wrote negatively about MacKay, particularly since Sands originally (in his first edition) produced a glowing tribute to the same person, but, within little more than a year (in his second edition), had changed his mind, perhaps as the result of a disagreement, but more probably because a positive assessment of the minister did not fit well with the developing overall theme of his book and especially the sharper focus of the second edition, which makes no secret of Sands' own sense of 'divine mission' to free the islanders from their many shackles.

The embattled MacKay had to endure the 'shipping in' of two successive, self-appointed spokespersons, with varying competencies in Gaelic, who took it upon themselves to present the ways, woes and wiles of St Kilda to the outside world, especially in an ecclesiastical context. As if one controversialist were not enough, Sands' literary *volt face* and searing criticism was followed ten years later by the particularly abrasive efforts of Robert Connell, whose deeply disparaging writing on the St Kildans, their church, their form of worship, their elders and especially their minister, plumbed the very nadir of bad taste,

---

11. Robson, *St Kilda: Church, Visitors and 'Natives'* opens this and other discussions by providing broad perspectives on the alleged 'peculiarities' of St Kilda.

12. Robson, *St Kilda*, 520.

even by today's tabloid standards.[13] Sands' literary labours seem tame and even bland by comparison. Connell, a Special Correspondent with the *Glasgow Herald*, arrived in St Kilda in October 1885, on board Captain John McCallum's steamship *Hebridean*, when she made an emergency dash to Village Bay with supplies to make up losses which the islanders had sustained in a serious storm. His later effusions must have confirmed amply MacKay's view that journalists like Connell were indeed possessed by the Evil One. Whatever MacKay's supposed deficiencies may have been, he certainly did not lack the ability to recognise a mischief-maker when he met him, or to make his own feelings abundantly clear. As a consequence, there is more than a whiff of personalised polemic in the air and the crackle of a fire-and-brimstone confrontation between 'principalities and powers', when the *Glasgow Herald* journalist describes (or, more accurately, vilifies) the minister. MacKay, it would seem, was not a 'push-over', nor was he prepared to do the bidding of the self-important 'great white chiefs' who had stepped ashore in his domain and who immediately embarked on what amounted to a challenge to his authority. 'The last person off the boat' was not going to run *his* island.[14] Unfortunately, MacKay's encounter with Connell was followed by a serious illness, possibly a stroke, which some of his congregation ascribed (perhaps with justification) to the impact of highly pejorative newspaper diatribes which he and the St Kildans had had to endure.[15]

---

13. Connell, *St Kilda and the St Kildians.*

14. This sentence echoes a saying heard by the writer in Mull when he visited the island in the 1990s, namely 'The last person off the boat runs the island!'

15. Connell describes MacKay's illness with gleeful humour which seems extremely inappropriate in the context.

If MacKay was reluctant to countenance his visitors' opinions and their desire for instant and total recognition, readers and writers beyond St Kilda were, in due time, glad to give them the centre-stage status that they craved, and to damn MacKay in like manner. The authority assigned to Sands and other 'external' writers by more recent commentators confirms eloquently the St Kildans' lack of status in literary evaluation; the external, non-Gaelic, non-St Kildan voice is everywhere dominant. External observers are 'privileged' over indigenous observers, who assume 'subaltern' roles, assisting the narrative from the sidelines, with occasional Gaelic quotations, rather than creating it from the centre. In postcolonial terms, the position of St Kilda is that of a microcosmic 'dominated' region, which has been subjected to 'imperial' and 'colonial' modes of external governance and interpretation. Indeed, it could be said that, in the process of 'interpreting' St Kilda, popular writers, unaware of their own limitations relative to accessing the 'natives' in their own language(s) and on their own terms, have constructed what may perhaps be termed 'St Kilda-ism', with an almost insuperable range of 'blind spots', on much the same lines as some western commentators have allegedly created 'Orientalism', as analysed and defined by the innovative (but contested) studies of Edward W. Said.[16]

Within Said's model, the 'silence' of the 'Other' (in the form of St Kilda or the Orient) is normal, if not normative, and a form of 'literary imperialism' takes over, which continues to subject the relevant 'puppet region' to the string-pulling of external adventurers. It may indeed be debated whether popular books by writers such as Steel and MacLean (and their nineteenth-century predecessors) relate to the 'real St Kilda' as known by its inhabitants, or whether

---

16. Said, *Orientalism*; for discussion of later reactions to Said's thesis, see Macfie, *Orientalism*.

they represent an 'alternative' or 'parallel' St Kilda which, inter alia, allows them (and their readers) to pursue their own theories, their likes and dislikes, with impunity.[17] Among the 'dislikes', the form of Christian faith and expression practised in St Kilda, pre-eminently after 1800, takes pride of place. Unfortunately for the 'dislikers', the 'voice' of native St Kildans, which is audible when 'St Kilda [eventually] writes back',[18] challenges and contradicts the negative interpretation favoured within the general run of works inclined towards 'St Kilda-ism'. The conflict between what is 'normal' and 'tolerable' to the islander, but 'abnormal' and 'intolerable' to the outside observer or 'incomer', intent on finding difference, is immediately apparent, and nowhere more graphically illustrated than in the case of St Kilda.

Seeing faith in context

It requires to be made clear that, in addition to the fundamental challenges enumerated above, a number of other factors contribute to the manner in which the Christian faith – in any context – is evaluated and its impact assessed by writers, and that

---

17.   The manner in which 'St Kilda', 'real' and 'imagined', has been, and continues to be, memorialised is reminiscent of the massive literary 'bubble' surrounding the tragedy of the RMS *Titanic*, which struck an iceberg on her maiden voyage in April 1912. The 'real' *Titanic* – the outstanding product of superb marine engineering – now has to struggle for space alongside the 'imagined' *Titanic*, which sails ever onwards (or downwards) in endless books, films, etc., with a plethora of theories, far-fetched ideas about the sinking, etc. St Kilda and the *Titanic* have a 'sad ending', which somehow has added to their mystique, and has been, perhaps, conducive to their ceaseless memorialisation. See Howells, *Myth of the Titanic*.

18.   This phrase echoes that of Salman Rushdie, '...the Empire writes back to the Centre...', used in the title of Ashcroft et al., *The Empire Writes Back*.

this consideration has a direct bearing on how church and faith in St Kilda are presented. Among these factors are:

(a) *The assessor's own espousal, or rejection, of the Christian faith, or of particular expressions of that faith.* An assessor who is broadly agnostic or atheistic is more likely to be 'hostile', unless s/he has learned to maintain neutrality of approach, and to identify 'minuses' as well as 'pluses'. Conversely, an assessor (like the present writer) who is already within a 'faith group', or linked to it, is more likely to be 'friendly' to the Christian faith, although s/he also requires to recognise the 'minuses' as well as the 'pluses', particularly in cultural contexts. In other words, despite different starting-points of enquiry, researchers ought to be able to find a 'middle ground' where it is possible to agree about gains and losses to people and society. In the case of St Kilda, it is unquestionably clear that, in the 'popular' works, the negative interpretation has prevailed, due in large measure to an in-built 'spin', stemming (apparently) from the writers' own rejection of the Christian faith, or a deep dislike of certain expressions of that faith, as well as their dependence on nineteenth-century writers who were 'hostile' (through 'ignorance') to the St Kildans' forms of worship. Writers who belong to a heavily 'ritualised' Christian tradition (Roman Catholicism, Anglicanism etc.) will find it hard to identify with the allegedly 'bleak' expression of 'personalised' faith within Scottish Presbyterianism, represented by very plain architecture, very basic furnishings, lack of images etc. in church buildings (like that in St Kilda, which often gave rise to derogatory comment). Further grounds for disagreement over the impact of the Christian faith on a particular society will be fostered by the division between 'moderates/traditionalists' and 'evangelicals' within Anglicanism and Presbyterianism.

(b) *Academic/theoretical schools of thought and discipline.* It is noticeable that a considerable chasm exists between secular anthropologists, on the one hand, and historians of Christian mission, on the other. The latter, though sometimes justly critical of mistakes and misunderstandings on the part of Christian missionaries, especially in the earlier phases of their endeavours, maintain a broadly favourable approach to overall patterns.[19] Anthropological evaluation, on the other hand, is usually markedly hostile to Christian mission, producing unfavourable assessments of the impact of missionary outreach to the Alaskan Inuit[20] and South Sea islanders,[21] for example, and highlighting the failure of missionaries to understand, or reach an accommodation with, traditional pre-Christian cosmologies. It is also argued fairly commonly by anthropologists that missionary 'intrusion' creates such serious dislocation of traditional practices that it leads to loss of identity, social breakdown and perhaps even the eventual destruction of the original community. Anthropology shows considerable interest in 'pre-contact' societies, and also in the factors that cause a 'puncturing' of these societies, resulting in their assimilation to the norms of 'external' cultures. Pre-contact societies may be seen as 'utopian' by some anthropologists, and this line of

---

19.   The best known general work is Neill, *A History of Christian Missions.*

20.   Fienup-Riordan, *Eskimo Essays*, offers a fascinating evaluation of Christian missionaries at work among the Yup'ik, 69 ff.

21.   An overview of Christian mission in Australasia and the Pacific is provided in Hastings, *A World History of Christianity*, 508–535. For a less matter-of-fact account, which may explain why those with a knowledge of the South Sea Islands (but not of the wider Highlands and Islands) will evaluate the Christian faith in St Kilda with some hostility, see Pettifer and Bradley, *Missionaries*, 31–52.

thinking appears in books about St Kilda, especially that by Charles MacLean, which was originally sub-titled 'Utopian St Kilda and its passing'.

(c) *Breadth of perspective.* It is very clear that the emphasis given to the 'unusual' or 'phenomenal' dimensions of the expression of the Christian faith in a particular context is in proportion to writers' awareness of, and familiarity with, patterns elsewhere within broader communities. An 'isolationist' tendency can be detected in anthropological studies, for example, in which close examination of a single community (naturally) encourages the identification of the 'distinguishing features' of that community, including its religious life. These 'distinguishing features' may be much less remarkable if set alongside practices commonly followed elsewhere. This is evident in the case of St Kilda, where the allegedly 'extreme' or 'harsh' forms of Christian expression identified by assessors as characteristic of St Kilda are also to be found within the wider Hebridean archipelago, and are not always regarded as 'extreme' or 'harsh' by those who are accustomed to, and who also respect and live by, these conventions. To them, these forms of worship are normal.

Different aspects of these positions will be more than apparent in the remainder of this paper, in the context of quotations from the relevant historiography. To set matters in context, we begin with broader perspectives on interpretations of the Christian faith beyond St Kilda, and then focus on the statements of writers who evaluate or describe the practice(s) of the faith in St Kilda itself.

1. Early missionary perceptions ('faith and flag' era)

Thèid an Soisgeul le sholas mar ghrèin
A dh'ionnsaigh an iar mun cuairt
Ameireaga, 's Innseanaich fhiat',
Is Eileanaich cian a' chuain;
Tàid aineolach, allaidh gun chiall,
Tàid buaireasach, fiadhaich, coirbt',
Tàid dìorrasach, dìoghaltch, dian,
Bras, àrdanach, iargalt', borb.

The Gospel with its light like the sun
Will move to the west and surround
America, and timid Indians,
And the remote Islanders of the sea;
They are ignorant, wild, without sense,
They are contentious, untamed, corrupt,
They are dogged, vengeful, headlong,
Unrestrained, proud, surly and rude.

This verse occurs in a Gaelic song composed about 1819 by the Rev. James MacGregor, a native of Comrie, Perthshire, who emigrated to Pictou, Nova Scotia. His emigration evidently heightened his awareness of contemporary overseas missionary enterprise, following the establishment of the London Missionary Society in 1795. The latter had a particular interest in the South Sea Islands, in the Pacific Ocean.[22] In his song, MacGregor took a broad sweep through missionary activities, beginning with the Highlands of Scotland, but embracing many other parts of the world, including the South Sea Islands, whose inhabitants are described above as 'Eileanaich cian a' chuain' ('the remote Islanders of the sea'). The verse reflects the 'triumphalist'

22.   See previous reference.

missionary vision of the age, and likens the Christian Gospel to the sun, making its illuminating and unstoppable progress across the benighted globe.[23]

The song is relevant to several aspects of the post-1800 evangelisation of St Kilda, including the approach of later writers (among them Steel and MacLean), if only to emphasise some important, contrasting perspectives. First, it shows unquestionably that Gaels themselves were caught up in the missionary fervour of their day. It was not a simple matter of innocent Gaels being 'gate-crashed' by (culturally) external do-gooders. Among these very same Gaels, and more than thoroughly familiar with contemporary Gaelic society, was the Rev. John MacDonald of Ferintosh, who arrived at Glen Bay, St Kilda, in 1822, and brought what later St Kildans called 'the true Gospel' to the islands. MacDonald wrote a journal in English, describing his visit (as he did on subsequent occasions until 1830),[24] but he also composed a long narrative poem in Gaelic, which sets out his main concerns in preaching to the St Kildans. His theology and homiletic style were much the same as he employed in other parts of Scotland, and it cannot be claimed that the St Kildans were singled out for some sort of 'punishment', as writers like MacLean might have it. His aim was to explain to the St Kildans salvation through Christ. Contrasting himself with contemporary gold-prospectors who would not shirk from world-wide searches for transient treasures, MacDonald felt a deeply personal responsibility to preach the enduring treasure of the Gospel to the St Kildans, and his intentions were already settled before he received a formal invitation from the Scottish SPCK to visit St Kilda:

---

23. Meek, 'Craobh-sgaoileadh'.
24. Kennedy, *Apostle of the North*, 66–118.

'Is cò nach seirmeadh an naidheachd
O èirigh gu luidhe na grèin'?
O, cò ach esan nach d'fhairich,
''S nach d'aithnich a cumhachd e fèin?'[25]

*'And who would not have proclaimed the message from
the rising to the setting of the sun? Who but the person
who had not himself experienced or acknowledged its
power?'*

Second, MacGregor's song indicates that missionaries, on the whole, believed that the inhabitants of remote areas were basically 'uncivilised' prior to the arrival of evangelical Christianity. However, John MacDonald did not use such terminology of the natives of St Kilda, to whom he was united by a common language (Gaelic) and a common culture, which extended across the western and northern Highlands, and all the other islands of the Hebrides. His desire was to bring the St Kildans into the fold of the wider family of faith in the Highlands and Islands, and not to demean them or to exclude them, by regarding them as idiosyncratic or 'far out'.

Nevertheless, certain 'external', non-Gaelic commentators on the spiritual state of the St Kildans in the first half of the nineteenth century were prone to treat the islanders on much the same basis as MacGregor viewed the South Sea islanders – the 'natives' needed to be approached cautiously, and before being admitted to the ordinances of the Christian faith (most notably communion), their spiritual state required to be investigated closely. Thus, before agreeing to accompany the Rev. Dr Norman MacLeod to St Kilda in 1838, the Rev. Dr David Dickson of St Cuthbert's, Edinburgh, 'who acted as controller of the S.P.C.K. Society', was anxious to ensure that

25. Dòmhnullach, *Marbhrainn*, 109.

> *the people are in such a state of preparation for being admitted to communion as to be ready without any previous preparation, except on the Saturday, or it may be on the Sabbath morning, to join in the service ... Unless however, I am satisfied in regard to this point, anxious as I am to visit the sphere of Mr. Mackenzie's labours, I cannot conscientiously do so with the special view of seeing the first administration of our Lord's Supper, supplied to the members of his flock. Satisfy me then, my dear sir, as to this, and all will be right...*[26]

Dickson's attitude to the St Kildans led MacLeod's biographer, his son the Rev. John MacLeod, to comment:

> *The worthy doctor seemed to be labouring under the impression that the simple-hearted natives of St. Kilda were a recently converted tribe of savages, instead of what those acquainted with them knew them to be – a pious people, simple in faith, reverent in devotion, pure in life...*[27]

In the event, Sunday 29 June 1838 turned out to be '*a day full of interest and a red-letter day in the scanty annals of the natives of St. Kilda*', and fifteen were admitted to the sacrament of communion which was celebrated in the afternoon.[28] The contemporary evidence shows that Gaelic-speaking clergymen from parishes beyond St Kilda were entirely 'at home' in Hirta, and at one with the ministry of the Rev. Neil MacKenzie. More importantly, the Christian faith had been embraced by the St Kildans in much the same way, and in the same form, as it had been internalised in other parts of the Highlands, and thus any notion of a progressive 'civilising' of supposed savages in a 'remote' part of the world is

26. MacLeod, *Memorials*, 156.
27. Ibid., 157.
28. Ibid., 160–63.

erroneous and misguided. The proper context in which to view the St Kildans and their church is that of the Scottish Highlands and the other islands of the Hebrides. To miss that perspective is to miss almost everything that matters.

Even so, the notion that St Kilda was somehow out on a limb, in both spiritual and secular matters, and comparable with the South Sea Islands, has continued into late twentieth-century writing, thus opening the field to potential misunderstanding and unhelpful comparisons, as well as 'contestable' sub-texts. Charles MacLean's 'utopian' argument occasionally alludes to the South Sea Islands, and specifically to Tahiti – a part of the world which has created heated debate about the influence of the Christian faith on indigenous islanders.[29] The role of Christian missionaries in the South Sea Islands is regularly condemned by anthropologists.

2. Present-day anthropologists' perceptions

The Protestant Church was the focus of much community life, for church-going and related activities structured much of the leisure time of the villagers. Church affairs were second in importance only to making a living. The pastor was an influential figure in the community, deeply involved in local decision-making and the arbiter of family morality. He preached against drunkenness, adultery, gambling, and any form of anti-family behavior. On the surface, the stern Puritan ethic of the early missionaries, with its implicit threats of hellfire and damnation for sinners, had profoundly affected village life. This ethic had struck hard from the beginning ... In the 1890s, another visitor wrote that the atmosphere was tinged by melancholy. [They] were

---

29.   MacLean, *Island on the Edge of the World*, 172.

forbidden to dance, and seemed bored and listless. They
were no longer happy and carefree. It was as if life had no
meaning for them. The conversion of the islanders led to a
general breakdown of meaning and purpose, and then to
demoralization.[30]

So writes the anthropologist, Brian M. Fagan, when discussing
Tahiti – and not, in fact, St Kilda! Nevertheless, this passage
would stand as a very passable summary of how the role and
influence of the Christian faith in St Kilda have been assessed
by twentieth-century 'popular' historians. The 'structuring' of
life in St Kilda by the Protestant Church (instead of 'the wind
and the waves') is a recurrent 'gripe' in their works. Likewise, the
dictatorial figure of the 'missionary' can be matched in popular
stereotypical portrayals of the Rev. John MacKay, and the notion
that the Christian Gospel offers nothing but 'threats of hellfire
and damnation for sinners' is rife in such writing. Again, the
idea that 'melancholy' replaces happiness is commonplace in
evaluations of St Kilda, and equally recurrent is the view that
'the conversion of the islanders led to a general breakdown of
meaning and purpose'. In the case of St Kilda, evacuation is
portrayed as being somehow a consequence, at least in part, of
the St Kildans' espousal of a particularly bleak and corrosive
brand of Christianity which destroyed their self-confidence, and
even their ability to cultivate their crops. Although there is no
firm evidence to support this view, it is nevertheless trotted out
regularly, or strongly implied, in twentieth-century and more
recent works, such as that of Haswell-Smith (below).

The fact that a closely similar assessment of how the Christian
faith affected the St Kildans can be found in the context of Tahiti
should put us on our guard against accepting that assessment

---

30. Fagan, *Clash of Cultures*, 186

as a so-called 'historical' analysis which is true to the actual experience of the St Kildans (rather than the perceptions of anthropologists or historians). It is more likely to be based on a 'critical' template or 'operating paradigm' which is common among secular anthropologists. If the paradigm or the template exists, there is a danger that 'facts' will be found to fit it – and that those which do not fit will be left aside or played down.

3. The Highland and Hebridean context

The penetration of evangelicalism had positive effects on Highland society. Deep religious experiences, through the revivals, gave people a new sense of self-worth which aided their physical survival. They used that renewed confidence to fight against some of the injustices perpetrated against them by landlords during the period known as the 'Highland Clearances' ... There were negative dimensions too. The eventual triumph of evangelicalism provided something of a doctrinal straitjacket, which, while encouraging the use of the secular culture as a vehicle for certain aspects of evangelicalism, set very clear limits to cultural, social and political involvement.[31]

Even if twentieth-century popular writers do see St Kilda through the lens of the South Sea Islands, and even if it can be argued that, on the contrary, St Kilda fits much more comfortably with the religious experience of the Scottish Highlands and Islands, there is still room for considerable, properly-nuanced debate about the pluses and minuses of that experience, in St Kilda as elsewhere. In fact, in a manner not dissimilar to what has happened to St Kilda, certain Highland historians, literary

---

31.   Meek, *The Scottish Highlands*, 34.

critics, poets and prose-writers have regarded the Christian faith as a malevolent and corrosive force at certain levels, broadly detrimental to indigenous Gaelic culture within the wider area.[32]

Because of the relative wealth of literary and other kinds of Gaelic evidence available for the Highlands and Islands as a whole, however, it is possible to evaluate whether such a perception is fair. As time and circumstances allowed in the 1990s and the early 2000s, I myself tried to assess the 'positives' and 'negatives' in this difficult field. The above quotation, which commits me somewhat uncomfortably to self-citation, reflects my overall deduction, namely that it was possible to arrive at a balanced conclusion, which emphasised the many benefits which came to the region as a result of the arrival of the Christian faith in various forms, especially after 1560. It would be both incorrect and unfair, however, to argue that the faith brought nothing but benefits, any more than it would be disingenuous to claim that it brought nothing but disadvantages; certain aspects of the secular culture were rightly challenged by the Protestant (and evangelical) church, but others, including the Gaelic language itself, were not always given the opportunity to thrive happily within an ecclesiastical context, which tended to favour English. Even so, the overall picture was not at all one of doom, gloom and destruction for Gaelic language and culture. It is beyond question that the Protestant church greatly aided the development of Gaelic literature and literacy, for example, even if the prescribed diet of reading was of a 'puritan' kind.

Another important conclusion of my studies was that, in many contexts, secular and sacred dimensions of society co-existed much more happily than many critics were prepared to admit. Secular songs and tales were often preserved within devout

---

32. Ibid., 58–64.

evangelical families, although these traditions were relegated to a relatively low position within these families' order of priorities. It is no accident that some of Gaelic Scotland's finest poets and writers were brought up within, or alongside, evangelical communities or families, which, from time to time, they were prepared to criticise somewhat strongly, while recognising the stimulus that such communities or families had given to their minds and intellects. They were certainly not denied the opportunity to interact with secular Gaelic culture, though limits may have been set to that interaction.[33]

For St Kilda, it is commonly argued that the arrival of the evangelical faith after 1822 seriously damaged, or even destroyed, the store of songs and stories within the community. This was not the case. Whatever may have been lost, much survived. In fact, it would seem that St Kilda matched the wider Highland experience in this respect, as in others. St Kilda's story-telling tradition was alive and well in the twentieth century, as evidence from the beginning and middle of that century shows. The evidence for the early twentieth century is found in the diaries of Mrs Alice MacLachlan, wife of Peter MacLachlan, the Mull-born missionary in St Kilda from 1906 to 1909. In her entry for Wednesday 1 April 1908, Mrs MacLachlan writes:

Lovely day. Had Finlay Mor, Ian Bahn [sic] and old Donald McQuien in ceilidhing and got great fun. Donald was in great form and was telling us heaps of stories about the islands – pirates etc. I wished I had had more Gaelic to understand better. He told us about men falling over the rocks at Soay – boys being stolen away from Boreray, and robbers coming to the island. His gestures were so funny and if any of the others dared to dispute anything he said

---

33. Ibid., 34–53.

> *he almost devoured them. Entertained them to supper and*
> *gave Ian Bahn his 'McCheyne', also presented others with*
> *'Grace Abounding' in Gaelic. They were delighted. No boats*
> *in.*[34]

Here is a picture of a ceilidh-house of the traditional kind, complete with gesticulating storyteller, flourishing in St Kilda in the early twentieth century – within the walls of the manse, no less! The 'pirate stories' told to Mrs MacLachlan remained an integral part of St Kildan memory until the early 1960s, when they were recorded by the School of Scottish Studies from Lachie MacDonald and his contemporaries. The recordings were played and discussed by Dr Cathlin Macaulay in her important presentation to this conference. It is also fascinating, and consistent with the wider Highland picture, that Gaelic translations of Robert Murray McCheyne's sermons, and of Bunyan's classic, *Grace Abounding to the Chief of Sinners*, were presented to the participants. No better evidence could be found of sacred and secular co-existing comfortably in a Gaelic context – indeed, this is one of the finest examples of such evidence that I have found for the Highlands and Islands as a whole.

Mrs MacLachlan was, of course, honest enough to draw attention to her inadequate command of Gaelic, which impoverished her understanding of the tales. It is clear, however, that she learned a great deal of Gaelic while in St Kilda. Part of the problem for St Kilda historiography has been, and remains, the egregious fact that few of the writers of the most influential books about the archipelago had any knowledge whatsoever of Gaelic beyond some words and phrases – and were apparently totally unaware of their serious deficiency in understanding

---

34.   Quine, *St Kilda Portraits*, 91.

Gaelic culture as a whole, and St Kilda as a part of that whole. It should also be noted that they have paid relatively little attention to Mrs MacLachlan's excellent and insightful diaries, even though these were written in English. If we add to this their lack of understanding of church and society in the wider Highlands and Islands, we can see quite clearly why St Kilda, in this matter at least, has been 'particularised' into a highly problematic community 'on the edge of the world'. The problems, however, did not lie in St Kilda.

4. St Kildans' writings about their church and faith – an inside view

The puritanical form of religion practised on St Kilda has often been interpreted by outsiders as austere and draconian, but Gillies' account of the islanders' religious practices makes clear the important role that these had in reinforcing the spiritual stamina of the community.[35]

As 'external' writings about St Kilda have been 'privileged' in previous assessments of church and faith, it seems only fair to reverse the order on this occasion and to give priority to 'internal' accounts by natives of St Kilda, or by individuals who spent several years in the main island of Hirta. The latter would include missionaries, their wives and children.

Through the outstanding efforts of David A. Quine, and most recently through the publication of books by the Rev. Donald John Gillies and Calum MacDonald (part of whose writing had already been published by David Quine in 1988), it is possible to access the perspectives of indigenous islanders to a degree that was probably not possible when Steel and MacLean were

---

35.   Gillies, *The Truth about St Kilda*, Rearword.

compiling their books. Both Gillies' and MacDonald's books were published posthumously, and both serve different purposes. Gillies' book, which combines autobiography with sermons, newspaper cuttings and general observation, is a much-needed attempt by a native St Kildan to set the record straight in matters of church and faith, while MacDonald's book is predominantly autobiographical, although it refers on several occasions to religious practices in these islands.

Despite their differing aims, however, both books have important points in common. First, they were written by native St Kildans who lived in the twentieth century, and whose experience covered a significant proportion of the period prior to the evacuation of 1930. This period is inadequately covered in the 'popular' histories of St Kilda, in which there is a tendency to 'stretch' the material relating to the Rev. John MacKay far beyond its proper place in the second half of the nineteenth century, and to use it as the benchmark for the entirety of the 'St Kildan experience'. Second, whatever the impact of MacKay's ministry may have been in its own time, it is more than evident that it was of little, if any, significance to Gillies or MacDonald; it had receded far into the mists, and both writers, from their differing vantage points, regarded the Christian faith of their community as totally normal, and also beneficial in their own formation as adults. There is nothing in their books which would lead us to believe that the Christian faith was a gloomy cloud which, like the mist on Conachair, had cast a baleful shadow over the village below. Indeed, to them it was quite the opposite – like a ray of sunshine piercing the clouds, it illuminated and guided the personal and corporate affairs of family and community in a healthy, wholesome manner.

A. Rev. Donald John Gillies

Gillies makes the following points, which may be summarised very briefly here, as they are extensive and readily accessible in his book (page numbers in brackets: see also the chapter on Gillies in this volume):

(i) Faith strengthened family cohesion within homes (1).

(ii) Evangelicalism ('the one true faith') offered a new starting-point when Dr John MacDonald arrived [in 1822]. MacDonald provided ecclesiastical infrastructure, i.e. church, manse etc. (2, 32–33).

(iii) Church provided education (5), including a small range of reading material in Gaelic, e.g. Bible, McCheyne, Boston, *Pilgrim's Progress* (39, 50), and missionaries' wives were teachers (39).

(iv) Missionaries were involved in technical matters, e.g. radio (10).

(v) Church arranged relief supplies [1885] (22–23).

(vi) Communion provided a focal point of celebration and mental stimulation for the community (25–27).

(vii) Rites of passage (birth, marriage, death) were solemnised by the church (27–28).

(viii) Faith produced men, women and leaders of exemplary conduct and character (29–30).

(ix) Missionaries assisted population in negotiating with Government, e.g. Dugald Munro prior to 1930 evacuation (37).

(x) Sabbath-keeping was strongly enforced (38–39).

B. Calum MacDonald

1. *My earliest recollection as a boy is a very happy one, having a very religious upbringing in a very happy home atmosphere, as Christianity was the basic standard of family life. The first*

thing every morning was family worship and prayer, and again at night before retiring to bed. No one dare lie or go to bed before family worship took place, unless they were ill. Sundays were strictly observed as the Lord's Day. There was a morning service at eleven a.m., Sunday school at three p.m., followed by an evening service at 6 p.m. No work of any kind was done on Sunday, except cooking your meals. Even the water was drawn from the wells on the Saturday and to store in pails to last all the Sabbath day. One was allowed to roam the hills and glens in between services and we, the youth of the village, would climb the hills and look over the cliffs at the birds which nested there and on the rocks, far down below, in their thousands, but we were not allowed any kind of play.[36]

2. My father was very religious, as was my mother. On Sundays it was his duty to ring the church bell, calling the villagers to the church service, and he was also the 'Precentor' who led the congregation's singing in Gaelic. My father was always the last to leave the church, and in the winter he had to light the paraffin lamps before the service and extinguish them when the service was over. After the rest of the congregation had gone home, I sat in our pew till all the lights were out and my father had lit the storm lantern. My father would then tell me to kneel beside him while he prayed, then he would ask me to say the Lord's Prayer in Gaelic. After, we would walk hand in hand home, which was about half a mile from the church. My reason for stopping behind to accompany him was that in my boyish mind, I thought I would be of some comfort to him in the dark, after being told so many ghost stories, which, as a child, I truly believed.[37]

---

36. MacDonald, *From Cleits to Castles*, 2.

37. Ibid., 4.

3. [A fishing-trip to Dùn is the context for this passage. When the lines were set, the fishermen rowed into a cave to spend the night. Young Calum was on his first trip of this kind.] *After supper was ended and packed away, the bible was taken out. We all started to sing a psalm and it reminded me of the church as the sound echoed throughout the cave. Most of the birds took fright and abandoned their nests, not to return until the service was over. After a chapter from the New Testament was read, we all knelt on the bottom of the boat and my father said evening prayers. Afterwards we rose up and climbed into our sleeping bags. We were packed like sardines, head to feet … During the night I could not sleep one wink. I could hear snoring from the others in the boat and the din from the birds was indescribable. The sea was lapping against our boat as we circled around our anchor and with my general excitement sleep was an impossibility.*[38]

The writings of Gillies and MacDonald demonstrate clearly that the Christian faith had been indigenised in St Kilda. As described by Gillies, its central rituals were wholly at one with those known elsewhere in Presbyterian contexts in the Highlands and Islands. The church was the intellectual and creative 'power-house' of the community, where expositions of the Bible and expressions of personal faith found their natural home. The influence of faith and church affected the whole of life, even as it was lived on the gannetries and in the boats. There is no indication that it was carried to the stacs as a 'talisman' of some kind; rather it was integral to the very core of the St Kildans. Within their understanding of the faith, they 'lived and moved and had their being.' It is fascinating too that MacDonald refers, in passing, to the 'many ghost stories' which he heard as a child – still another

---

38.   Ibid., 5.

indication that storytelling was alive and well in St Kilda in the early twentieth century, despite sweeping claims to the contrary by writers who were not themselves St Kildans.

C. Missionaries' relatives

4. *The church was a very simple place, rather austere, which matched the simple, robust faith of the folk who filled it each Sunday. There was no heating, but I don't remember that we ever complained of the cold. The St Kilda folk were grand churchgoers. Even babies of a few weeks old were taken to church; nobody stayed away unless they were ill ... In the winter, each family was lighted to the church by a hurricane lantern, or a ship's lantern; and these were carefully placed on the floor; with the flame turned down, until the service was over, when they were turned up for the homeward journey. There was something very comforting about the string of twinkling lights which pierced the darkness as the congregation walked home. I have never heard such hearty singing anywhere as in the church in St Kilda, and we had two excellent precentors in William MacDonald and Norman MacKinnon, both of whom have, alas, long since passed on.* Mary Cameron, *Childhood Days on St Kilda* [1919–26].[39]

5. *The St Kildans were rich in Christian faith and were rich in the graces that stem from that faith. Thus they lived together in unity, and their differences were of a minor nature incidental to living in such close proximity to each other. They were open and honest, mutually helpful, and generous to a degree, as we in the Manse were privileged to know.* Alexander MacLeod, son of John MacLeod, missionary and teacher in St Kilda, 1926–29.[40]

---

39. Quine, *St Kilda Portraits*, 190.
40. Ibid., 212.

The comments of those who belonged to missionary families corroborate the impressions of natives of St Kilda, like the Rev. Donald John Gillies and Calum MacDonald. For the thirty-year period from 1900 to 1930, we can conclude that the St Kildans enjoyed their church, practised their faith and were happy with their spiritual provision. The missionaries and their wives were central to the life of the island, providing basic medical services, education and a much-needed 'buffer' between the St Kildans and the outside world. Missionaries such as Peter MacLachlan, for example, also defended (successfully) trawler skippers when they were accused of fishing within the three-mile limit round St Kilda. In the early twentieth century, the manse offered the equivalent of a 'mission to deep-sea fishermen', by providing meals and support of different kinds for visiting crews, thus facilitating a broader 'communication network' for St Kilda itself. More generally, the St Kildans' post-1900 religious conventions, buildings and devotions can be matched without any difficulty in other Hebridean islands. They lived with the 'restrictions' of Sabbath observance, as did their fellows throughout the Highlands and Islands, but they were not inclined to complain bitterly about their supposedly unfortunate lot. Their perspectives, as indigenous islanders, stand in the sharpest possible contrast to those of the majority of new 'adventurers', 'literary tourists' and would-be 'liberators' who arrived in Village Bay in the last quarter of the nineteenth century, usually by steamship, to observe their habitat, and, wherever possible, to find fault with it and with them, and thus to reinforce their own superior status.

5. Visitors'/tourists' writings on St Kilda's church and ministers – an outside view

As we have already noted, two of the most influential 'literary tourists' of the nineteenth century made landfall during the long incumbency of the Rev. John MacKay, and their perceptions of his central role and 'rule' in the St Kildan community influenced not only their own writings, but also those of certain other writers down to the present day. To them, he was a stumbling-block, standing solidly in the way of the implementation of *their* high ideals, practising forms and rituals of church life which *they* did not recognise, and seemingly 'lording it' over a dispirited and abject people, so as to lead his flock astray (from the paths that the *visitors* thought they should follow). It is probably not too much to say that their writings are largely responsible for the creation of this St Kildan 'bogeyman', whose short stature and tall 'lum hat' were easy to caricature, and continue to cast a long, glowering shadow over Village Bay.

For John Sands, who first visited St Kilda in 1875, it was important to demonstrate to the outside world that the St Kildans were being exploited by institutional and other powers, among them their landlords and the resident minister of the Free Church. Sands regarded himself as 'a man with a mission' on his second visit to St Kilda in 1877:

> *To break open the door of MacLeod's prison was the object of my second visit to St Kilda. To liberate the poor serfs who had been so long incarcerated and cruelly used, and to bring them into communication with the rest of the world, was my mission, and often when rambling amongst the stern rocks on the tops of the mountains, or sitting listening to the solemn sound of the waves upon the shore, I felt as if I had had a divine call to perform the work, and must proceed at any cost, and despite of any opposition. Providence often selects strange instruments with which to execute His purposes, – instruments that would seem altogether unsuitable to Doctors Begg and McLauchlan.*[41]

---

41.   Sands, *Out of the World*, 1878, 122–3.

Sands' use of apocalyptic language, echoing Christ's first sermon, and his literary self-portrait as a latter-day Moses (receiving divine insight on the mountain tops) and as a romantic, almost Yeatsian ('Lake Isle of Innisfree') dreamer, allow us to understand why he collided with MacKay. It is also more than evident that Sands was unsympathetic to the Free Church of Scotland as a whole (represented by his references to the Revs. James Begg and Thomas McLauchlan), and it was therefore unlikely that the 'brand' found in St Kilda would be any better than that elsewhere. He regarded himself as a highly important 'authority figure', a 'man sent from God' in his own right – and St Kilda was too small for two such 'prophets'. One required to be eliminated, or at least knocked from his pedestal.

For Robert Connell, who had a vested interest in discovering how the St Kildans responded to external largesse in their alleged poverty and scarcity in the autumn of 1885, the islanders were essentially rogues and scroungers, pious frauds who had deceived their Scottish benefactors, and were blighted by a form of what he called 'socialism'. Having received supplies by deception (according to Connell), they were additionally so incompetent and selfish that they fell out about their distribution. They were people with few, if any, virtues, and the minister of the Free Church, in Connell's view, had contributed to their failings. Connell, therefore, chose to blacken the reputation of the entire population of the island; the minister is only one of many individuals who are pelted with vitriolic verbal slurry.

These are the overall aims which have to be kept in view in any fair-minded assessment of the 'evidence' provided by Sands and Connell on the matter of church and faith in St Kilda. Their writings are *not neutral* in intention or presentation; far from being neutral, each book has a distinct agenda, and the evidence is 'laundered' to suit. For many readers, nevertheless, these books were a first introduction to St Kilda, which most seemed to take at face value, with the result that echoes and reprises of Sands and Connell can be detected in numerous subsequent works. Given their nature, it is astonishing that these nineteenth-century 'damn and tell' volumes could have been invested with any value for (and by) post-1960 historians, beyond their undoubted significance as fascinating, if not at times horrifying, examples of what happened when highly literate visitors first landed on the shores of St Kilda, but were unable to relate to, or cope with, the reality of what they saw and heard. This was 'culture clash' at its most dramatic. Irresistible force met immovable object, and the wreckage from the resulting crash spilled into books and articles, with immense potential for inflicting collateral damage, down to the present day.

The work of Sands was followed by a response (1878) from George Seton, an Edinburgh advocate who visited the island briefly in July 1877, as one of the first passengers to be landed there by the *Dunara Castle*, when she inaugurated the annual summer steamship services to St Kilda. Thereafter, substantial books on St Kilda were published every decade or so, beginning with Connell (1887). The photographers, Richard and Cherry Kearton, visited St Kilda in 1896, and Richard Kearton published an important volume of photographs and commentary, *With Nature and a Camera* (1898). The century was rounded off with a book by Norman Heathcote (1900). There is a noticeable element of intertextual borrowing among the authors, with each later author referring to what the previous author(s) had written. All of them comment on the minister and church in St Kilda, but Seton, Kearton and Heathcote challenge or modify points made by Sands and/or Connell. George Seton, whose interest in St Kilda had been sparked by Sands, was the first to draw attention to the conflicting assessments of the Rev. John MacKay in Sands' 1876 and 1878 editions (see B. 4 below). In his 1898 book, *With Nature and a Camera*, Richard Kearton sowed seeds of doubt about the validity of Sands' description of the St Kildans as they went to church (See E. 8 below). It would seem that the 1870s and 1880s were, on the whole, the most 'dangerous' period in St Kilda's progressive journalistic exposure to the outside world, as writers like Sands and Connell were entering what to them was a completely alien world, and reacting accordingly. Possibly because St Kilda became less of a novelty as a result of summer-season steamship services, a more level-headed approach to the archipelago and its people gradually began to appear in books and newspapers after 1900, although the seminal writings of Sands and Connell continued to exert a strong influence on later (external) authors.

A. John Sands

1. *[The minister is] not only an earnest and honest man, but a kind-hearted one withal, whom those of any or of no persuasion would respect. There, posted like a sentinel on a rocky bank close to the sea, his whole aim is to keep the devil out of the island. Absorbed in this duty, he forgets the loneliness of his situation, and is deaf to the roaring of the waves that rage before his sentry-box during the long winter, and blind to the desolate aspect of the hills that tower steeply around, their lofty tops enveloped in drifting fogs. He is contented with plain fare and drinks none, is attentive to the infirm, and shares, in a stealthy way, what luxuries he has with them. Although an educated man, he has no books and no newspapers to enliven his solitude. Who is so anxious as he when the boats happen to be caught in a storm? Methinks I see him now, wandering restlessly on the shore, watching the waves outside the bay lashed into foam by the strong north wind, until the boats came round the rocky point ... Although a bachelor, he is seldom to be seen without a rose-cheeked urchin – a lamb of his flock – hanging on to his breeches-pocket and following*

him like a dog. Personally I am indebted to him for numberless acts of friendship, – kindness continued from first to last. He pressed me to live in the house, and when, preferring freedom and the bagpipes, I declined his invitation, he did his utmost to render me comfortable in my own quarters. Take him for all in all, the Free Kirk has few soldiers she has more reason to feel proud of.[42]

2. The best resident ruler, 'guide, philosopher, and friend,' for St Kilda would be a sensible, firm, and good-tempered old sailor, able to work and repair a boat, to teach the three R's and a little English to the young, and scrape a reel on the fiddle for the girls to dance to; and the worst home ruler would be a well-meaning but feeble-minded, irresolute, yet domineering fanatic, whose servant would lead him by the nose, and get him to preach at any woman to whom she had a spite, who would be obliged to sit and listen in silence, however innocent. This latter character is, of course, entirely supposititious, but it is quite possible that the Free Church might send such a representative to St Kilda, to sit like an incubus on the breast of the community. In that sequestered island, beyond the supervision of Sessions and Presbyteries, he might, by working on the religious prejudices of the flock, retain his grasp, and exercise a tyranny which would never be tolerated in other places.[43]

3. Now-a-days the whole population are members of the Free Church. They attend Divine service three times every Sunday, and hold a prayer meeting (which is conducted by the elders) every Wednesday evening. The Sabbath is indeed a day of intolerable gloom. At the clink of the bell the whole flock hurry to the church, with sorrowful looks, and eyes bent upon the

---

42. Sands, *Out of the World*, 1876, cited by Seton, *St Kilda Past and Present*, 269–70.

43. Sands, *Out of the World*, 1878, 115.

ground. It is considered sinful to look to the right hand or to the left. They do not appear like good people going to listen to glad tidings of great joy, but like a troop of the damned whom Satan is driving to the bottomless pit. Surely this is not the proper deportment for good Christians – surely religion, with its promises of remission of sins and everlasting life beyond the grave, should make true believers more cheerful and not more miserable than benighted heathen, who have no such consolations. Instead of assuming this dejected behaviour, it appears to me that real Christians should march with heads erect, with eyes beaming with exultation, and scorning to look upon the vile earth, and with glad voices singing, 'O death, where is thy sting? O grave, where is thy victory?'[44]

One can only wonder how the history of church and faith in St Kilda might have been presented to the outside world if Sands had adhered to his initial – very fine, and highly complimentary – portrait of the Rev. John MacKay, weathering the physical and spiritual storms of his island outpost. This initial sketch of MacKay fits very well with what is known about the functions of the manse and the missionaries in the early twentieth century. It should be noted, too, that even in his 'alternative portrait' of MacKay, Sands writes in a curiously oblique manner, comparing 'what is' with 'what should have been'. He uses his authorial persona to distance himself from his obvious criticism of MacKay, and deftly avoids what became a vicious tirade of abuse in the later writing of Connell. (It is perhaps noteworthy that some of the post-1960 historians confuse Connell with Sands.) In the final quotation from Sands, we witness his complete failure to understand the self-abasement which was, and remains, a characteristic of Christian believers' approach to worship in the Presbyterian

---

44.   Ibid., 29–30.

Highlands and Islands. It is not that these believers are joyless or miserable; it is that they are humbled by the realisation that they are going into the presence of the Lord God Almighty, and, for that reason, they do not wish to engage in an emotional, triumphalist round of self-expression, even when sure of their salvation. Sands, it would seem, had his own expectations of 'real Christians', which he set out with characteristic arrogance, but these expectations were not fulfilled in St Kilda. Nor would they have been fulfilled in any other parts of the north-west Highlands and Hebrides at that time.

B. George Seton

4. *Since October 1865, the Rev. John McKay, now about sixty years of age, has been the faithful bishop of St Kilda.*[45]

Seton then provides the quotation from Sands, 1876, given in A. 1 above, and concludes it with a wry footnote (270–71) beginning as follows: '*This eloquent panegyric is most unaccountably omitted from the second edition of Mr Sands's work, in which, however, there are several references to the minister of a somewhat less complimentary kind.*' He contrasts the uncomplimentary picture of 1878 with the highly favourable one of 1876, and finishes with the Latin tag, *Quantum mutatus ab illo Hectore.*

C. Robert Connell

5. *Mr. Mackay, who is a native of Jeantown, Ross-shire, and is turned seventy, has been pastor of the island since October, 1865. Never once since his appointment has he been off the island. His yearly stipend is £80. There can be no manner of doubt that for much of the unhealthy moral atmosphere pervading the island at present the ecclesiastical authority in*

---

45. Seton, *St Kilda Past and Present*, 269.

the person of Mr. Mackay is mainly responsible. The weak-minded pope and prime-minister rolled into one who rules the destinies of the island has reduced religion into a mere hypocritical formalism, finding no place in his creed for self-reliance or any of the manlier virtues. Men are enjoined to two hours devotions every week day, and eight on Sunday, when they must also wear a sad face and speak an octave under their usual voice. Whistling and singing are at all times tabooed, and not to comply is to be accounted an infidel, and worse than a heathen. The apostle of this novel evangel has no stomach for the common affairs of life. He has enervated the islanders by arrogating to himself all power, temporal as well as spiritual, and with this influence, which might have been directed to the most useful ends, Mr. Mackay has only sought to enforce a fantastical sacerdotalism. It is nothing to Mr. Mackay whether the poor people starve on their crofts or neglect the fishing so long as his own silly fads are observed. There is no use blinking the fact that during the twenty years the Reverend gentleman has held the island in his firm grip no useful public work of any kind has been executed. We know something of what he might have succeeded in doing. At every point in the island one comes upon the evidences of the practical usefulness of a former minister, the Rev. Neil Mackenzie, under whose beneficent guidance the St. Kildians appear to have put forth some energy to improve their condition. That, however, was in the good old days of cakes and ale, before the Disruption, when whistling was not as yet a sin, and when fiddling and piping, and even dancing, were not unknown in St. Kilda.[46]

6. *The name of our preacher was Donald McDonald. He is not an elder, but he is the most intelligent and sensible man on the island. The service was opened by the congregation singing in*

---

46. Connell, *St. Kilda and the St. Kildians*, 54–5.

Gaelic the first four verses of the 25th Psalm. In the absence of the precentor-beadle at Boreray, Donald had himself to lead the praise. The singing was got through in the last-century fashion, the conductor giving out line after line. I do not wish to be uncharitable but I state solemnly that I never heard such a medley of discordant, incongruous sounds. I can compare it to nothing but the baying of a pack of hyenas. There was no tune – or rather every man had a tune for himself, and where two happened to be in the one key it was an accident. It pained one to be compelled to listen. Praise over, Donald engaged in prayer. He prayed with evident fervour for the space of twenty minutes, the women all the while groaning and sighing, just as other members of the emotional sex do at Salvation Army meetings. Then came what was to serve as a sermon – an exposition of the 10th chapter of Romans. In this task Donald held out for half an hour. Following this, we had other four verses of the 25th Psalm, a long Prayer from an elder in a back seat, two more verses of the same psalm, another prayer from a man in a front seat, and yet two more verses of the same favourite psalm. Then came the passing round of the hat, and afterwards we were at liberty to go. The women rose first and left the church in a body; the men followed by themselves at a respectful distance.[47]

These quotations demonstrate the all-embracing nature of Connell's attempt to expose the 'unreconstructed' temper of the St Kildans, their faith, their worship and (especially) their minister. It would seem that the era of the Rev. Neil MacKenzie (1830–1843), who was instrumental in improving the housing stock of the St Kildans in 1836–38, was to Connell a somewhat romantic Golden Age, untrammelled by the excesses of the Free Church, represented

47.   Ibid., 85–6.

by the Rev. John MacKay. However, the distinction between 'then' and 'now', as set out in Connell's terms, is somewhat naïve. While it is true that MacKenzie did act in a thoroughly practical manner, consistent with the broader aims of Improvement, he was also largely responsible for developing the deep spirituality of the St Kildan people following the visits of the Rev. John MacDonald, who introduced MacKenzie to St Kilda in 1830. MacKenzie was, in fact, minister of St Kilda when the community experienced a very deep religious revival in 1841. This revival was part of a movement which was felt in the Hebrides more generally in that year – another pointer to the place of St Kilda within the wider Highland and Hebridean cultural area – and paved the way for acceptance of Free Church principles throughout the region.[48] The Free Church of Scotland was not forced down the throats of any communities in the Highlands and Islands; these communities, in St Kilda as elsewhere, were ready and waiting for the Free Church when it came. When he arrived in St Kilda in 1865, MacKay became the custodian of the spiritual legacy left by the Rev. Neil MacKenzie and the Rev. John MacDonald before him, a legacy which had been maintained largely by the people themselves for some twenty years before his arrival. However strict he may have been in his custodianship, MacKay was not responsible for implanting or consolidating the expression of the Christian faith which Connell and others discovered, to their deep discomfort, in St Kilda.

It is also questionable whether MacKay was as grimly unprogressive as he is painted by Connell. He may have been 'narrow', but in the matter of so-called 'progress' he had his predecessors and successors in a similar mould throughout the Highlands and Islands. They too stood for what they believed against all comers, and were 'strict' in their churchmanship. They did not see themselves as, nor were they appointed to be, 'local

---

48.   Meek, 'Gaelic Bible, Revival and Mission', 132.

development officers' in addition to their spiritual responsibilities. If they became involved in the social or political life of their communities, that was usually a matter of personal choice. It is certainly evident that MacKay did not avoid such issues, although he was unwilling to countenance some of the recommendations made by the bold, self-confident Sands, particularly with regard to establishing a trading link between St Kilda and Harris. In resisting Sands, he was surely correct – a point that is seldom, if ever, made by present-day writers. Yet it is equally evident that MacKay was wholly supportive of Sands' (eventually sensible) conclusion 'that nothing but a steamer would answer the purpose I had in view'.[49] To this end, MacKay arranged an *ùghdarras*, or mandate, on behalf of the St Kildans, dated 'the first month of Autumn, in the year 1876', for John Sands to act as their representative in obtaining a steamship service. The mandate was drawn up in Gaelic and English, and its Gaelic form is a tribute to MacKay's excellent command of the language and his gift for clear, concise expression. The mandate stresses that the steamer, by calling twice a year in April and October, would greatly aid *ar sonas agus soirbheachadh saoghalta* ('our worldly happiness and prosperity') – a perspective that immediately contradicts the common notion (deriving largely from Connell) that MacKay's principal concern was with the doctrinal and ecclesiastical rectitude of his oppressed flock, and that he was unconcerned about the worldly welfare of his people. John Sands took this responsibility in hand, and in July 1877 Martin Orme's *Dunara Castle* initiated the first St Kilda summer service. In his 1878 edition, however, Sands states that he was still struggling to fulfil the terms of the mandate, and there is no evidence that the arrival of the *Dunara Castle* was due solely to him.[50] He

49. Sands, *Out of the World*, 124.
50. Ibid., 138–42.

may, nevertheless, have had some influence with James 'Paraffin' Young, who had already provided a boat for the St Kildans and was known to be sympathetic to their plight, and whose wider family may also have had financial interests in Orme's company.[51] By then Young was living on his estate of Kelly in Wemyss Bay, not far from the home of Martin Orme in Bishopton. It is certainly clear that Sands helped to raise the profile of St Kilda at a critical time, and that the Rev. John MacKay assisted Sands in his desire to acquire a steamship service for St Kilda. It is not, however, by any means evident that Sands alone was the essential link in the chain which finally anchored a 'regular' steamship in Village Bay each summer from 1877 to 1939.[52]

Connell's account of the St Kildans' style of worship shows his deep contempt for all things St Kildan, as well as his inability to recognise his own lack of ecclesiastical or cultural understanding. Immediately, we are transported *from* St Kilda to an alien mental landscape, rooted in imperial concepts of remote 'natives' in their jungles on other continents, surrounded by 'discordant, incongruous sounds' and the 'baying of a pack of hyenas'. Here, however, the 'hyenas' are in church. These word-pictures are the verbal equivalents of John Sands' thoroughly contemptuous caricatures of St Kildan people, including the Rev. John MacKay, portrayed alongside fulmars and gannets. The steamships which conveyed Connell to St Kilda in 1885 brought other, later journalists, who found (or lost!) their literary bearings by means of Connell's efforts.

---

51.   Meek, *Steamships to St Kilda*.
52.   The fact that Sands and MacKay were, apparently, in complete agreement about the need for a steamship makes it all the more difficult to understand why Sands took against MacKay. A convergence of all interests is apparent in the St Kilda mandate entrusted to Sands.

D. Robert MacFarlan

7.   *Arrived in the bay opposite the dwelling-houses on the island,
     the ship cast anchor, and one of the small boats was lowered,
     and the passengers were taken ashore in groups of a dozen or
     more, the officers of the ship accompanying. Before we had
     got to shore, the natives had come down to meet us. They did
     not impress me favourably, and subsequent conversation and
     inquiry regarding them did not alter my first impression ... The
     minister is the Rev. John Mackay, the teacher is a Macrae, and
     the nurse is Mrs Urquhart. The minister is prophet, priest, king,
     policeman, judge and final arbiter. His long residence on this
     lonely island has assimilated him to the people, who have
     pulled him down quite as much as he has lifted them up. He,
     it seems, encourages the poor folks in their peculiar delusions
     and prejudices. In particular, he incites them to remain on
     the island, rather than strike out into the world, and make
     men and women of themselves by getting rid of their present
     humiliating condition. Just now they appear to be not a great
     deal above the level of professional beggars.*[53]

MacFarlan arrived at St Kilda on the steamship *Electric*, but,
although he had the opporunity to observe the St Kildans at first
hand, he was unable (perhaps because of the brevity of his visit)
to comprehend the dynamics of their community. Instead, he
summarised the perspectives of Robert Connell, and damned
the Rev. John MacKay accordingly. For MacFarlan also, MacKay
was an obstacle to progress, in opposing migration from St
Kilda. We may therefore conclude that MacKay believed that St
Kilda ought to remain inhabited, and, in that context, he has
been given very little credit for the longer-term survival of the
community in Village Bay. If MacKay had not been prepared to

---

53.   Robert MacFarlan, in *The Dumbarton Herald*, 1888.

'tough it out' in St Kilda for 24 years, covering a critical phase in the life of Hirta, when steamships were bringing to its shores men like Sands and Connell, as well as many other equally misinformed tourists and would-be philanthropists, the history of St Kilda might have been very different. It could well have ended in evacuation before 1900.

MacKay may have had his faults, but one of them was assuredly not a mere nodding acquaintance with the St Kildans, or a 'hit and run' attitude to St Kilda. He was ready for the 'long haul', and so too was the Free Church. He also survived the *ad hominem* diatribes in the press, which are without parallel in Hebridean history for their disparagement and, indeed, libellous content. Given that the government and other secular organisations cared little for St Kilda, and invested next to nothing in its maintenance, the Free Church of Scotland (and the United Free Church after 1900) surely also deserve fair recognition for providing leadership for the community, even if that leadership was not always to everyone's satisfaction.

E. Richard Kearton

8. *If Mr Sands faithfully recorded what he saw at this place in the 'seventies, when the people went to church "with sorrowful looks, and eyes bent upon the ground like a troop of the damned being driven by Satan to the bottomless pit," and no one spoke to another above a whisper, or looked to right or left without considering he had sinned, a very great improvement has taken place in the direction of reason and cheerfulness. Directly we got out of church, they all doffed their bonnets and shook hands with us, and such as were able to asked us how we were and chattered with us all the way up the path to our cottage.*[54]

---

54. Richard Kearton, *With Nature and a Camera*, 1898, 11.

It is significant that the warm reception given to Richard and Cherry Kearton was such as to make Richard Kearton raise a question about the accuracy of Sands' 1878 description of the 'sorrowful' St Kildans on their way to church.

6. External evaluations of the faith of the St Kildans 1970–2001

A. 'Popular' secular perspectives

1. *But [in contrast to Alexander Buchan] MacDonald, known and revered as the 'Apostle of the North' for his work in the Highlands, was a puritanical hard-necked evangelist … who earnestly set about the destruction of the island culture with all the zealous goodwill of a holy bigot … During his first eleven days in St Kilda, which unfortunately coincided with harvest-time, he preached to the inhabitants thirteen long sermons. The St Kildans took to this kind of punishment with enthusiasm and were filled with admiration for the man who meted it out. They lavished presents upon him and wept bitterly when he left them for the last time in 1830. But their admiration and respect were not returned. MacDonald was appalled by the moral condition of the islanders.* Charles MacLean.[55]

2. *The Rev. John Mackay, formerly a school teacher, who had been ordained expressly for the purpose of going to St Kilda, was an unmarried man of about fifty, with an alarming capacity for zeal. Shortly after his arrival on the island in 1865 he established a vibrantly harsh rule over his parishioners. Services on Sunday at eleven, two and six o' clock were made to last from two to three hours each, so that effectively the islanders spent the whole day in church. During the week a service, prayer meeting or period of religious instruction was*

---

55. MacLean, *Island on the Edge of the World*, 122–23.

held every day except Monday and Saturday. Mackay preached long, repetitious sermons in Gaelic, which invariably included the same message of hell-fire and eternal damnation to all sinners. Complete attention was demanded throughout these dim effusions, even of the very young. Charles MacLean.[56]

3. After Mackay left St Kilda in 1889 there was a slight improvement, but as late as the 1920s the islanders were going to church twice on Sundays, on the first Monday of every month and to a prayer meeting every Tuesday, with each service putting a stop to all work twelve hours on either side of it. Charles MacLean.[57]

4. As more enlightened missionaries came and went the oppressive cloud of salvationism was lifted a little, but the work of men like Mackay and the Apostle was never to be undone. The imposing of a strict, puritanical orthodoxy upon a people whose simple and vulnerable culture was delicately balanced within the complexities of a natural system, was as successful from one point of view as it was irredeemable from the other. The St Kildans made no attempt to resist the dogmatism that was forced upon them, and even as they watched it bring life on the island to a halt they accepted it as inevitable and right. They allowed fatalism to come uppermost and relaxed into deepest superstition, while their incentive for survival grew weak before the onset of disease and a lingering population crisis. Charles MacLean.[58]

5. Of all the influences brought to bear upon the minds of the people of Village Bay, that of religion played the greatest part in determining their destiny. For nearly five hundred years, the ministers and missionaries were the only educated people to live on the island for any great length of time. In their hands,

---

56. Ibid., 126–27.
57. Ibid., 128.
58. Ibid., 131–32.

therefore, lay the power to encourage good and create evil. After the Disruption of 1843 within the Church of Scotland, the stern faith of the Free Church, in the manner of its application and of its acceptance, made slaves of the people of St Kilda. The damage that was done in little over half a century of Free Church rule was to prove too great for the repairing zeal of latter-day missionaries like Dugald Munro .... Most [ministers] saw fit to pass on to their remote island flock their own personal prejudices and bigotry. On St Kilda, religion in the hands of some was to help stifle what little initiative existed among the inhabitants. Tom Steel.[59]

6. *From the time of MacDonald's crusade a marked change took place in the nature of the people of Village Bay. The St Kildans lost their sense of gaeity and their love of song and dance. Their way of life, previously governed by wind and tide, was thereafter subject to the demands of regular church-going. If the well-intentioned mission of the minister was a success, that success was due to the character of the islanders themselves. What MacDonald preached appealed to their superstitious nature. They believed implicitly in what he told them and a religion, the roots of which lay deep in the fear of the unknown, began its long domination over the minds of the people of St Kilda.* Tom Steel.[60]

7. *The other vital contribution to the eventual collapse of society on the island was the hell-fire and damnation of crusading Christian ministers. By far the most notorious was the Rev. John Mackay who was resident from 1865 to 1889. By the end of his evil ministry the islanders had been browbeaten into so much church attendance every day of the week that there was insufficient time for growing and gathering food.* Hamish Haswell-Smith.[61]

---

59. Steel, *Life and Death of St Kilda*, 1975, 92, 94.
60. Ibid., 95.
61. Haswell-Smith, *The Scottish Islands*, 317.

An obvious characteristic of the above quotations, apart from their dislike of the Christian faith itself and their debt to Sands and Connell, is their almost wholly derogatory range of vocabulary, which portrays evangelists as 'bigots', and the St Kildans as superstitious, fearful weaklings, unable to determine the future of their own community, and in thrall to the 'tyranny' of a deeply disempowering dogma, to the extent that they could not rearrange their work-schedules. By subscribing to evangelical Christianity, argue Steel and MacLean, they merely exchanged one form of superstition for another – surely a disparaging intellectual short-cut, which demeans the St Kildans. After MacKay's departure, according to MacLean, there is only a 'slight improvement' in their spiritual circumstances, and the stage is set for the *denoument* of evacuation. There is, however, no evidence known to the present writer, beyond a general, unsubstantiated assumption, that there was any *directly causal* link between the nature of the faith as practised by the St Kildans and the eventual evacuation of their island in 1930. Haswell-Smith's (apparently) thoughtless parroting of Connell, with a dash of modern MacLean thrown in, speaks for itself – somewhat sadly, it must be said, in a book published as recently as 2004, given that Robert MacFarlan (lacking the more detailed studies available to Haswell-Smith) did much the same in 1888.

Lack of proper steamship services, the growing allure of the mainland to young St Kildans after the First World War, and loss of manpower in the 1920s were identified by the St Kildans themselves (including the Rev. Donald John Gillies) as the principal causes of their ultimate dilemma, and we may surely credit them with knowing the real circumstances of their own final departure from their own island. Those who lived in the island, and who knew at first hand what was happening in their community, must be our best witnesses.[62] In any case, a

---

62. Gillies, *Truth about St Kilda*, 83–85.

personalised antipathy towards the faith of any group, Christian or otherwise, St Kildan or Tahitian, or towards a representative of that group, is not a credible foundation for intellectual argument, as it rests precisely on what Steel calls 'personal prejudices and bigotry'.

B. Scholarly pro-faith perspectives

8. *Although the St Kildans were not of a mind to sail out from or into their island on the Sabbath, they were not the legalists that Hebridean Sabbatarianists are portrayed as being. And even with the harrowing ordeals of their existence, there is every evidence that, far from being an unwelcome and unnecessary burden, the Free Church evangelicalism of the St Kildans was part of what fortified them in their harsh island life.* Rev. I. D. Campbell.[63]

9. *In capturing the spiritual high ground, the islanders disrupted a key component of the tourist experience. The tactical response of many travellers was to characterise the St Kildans as being fanatical and extremist, a line which twentieth-century writers have happily reproduced. Although the practice of worship in St Kilda was not substantially different from the evangelicalism of other Gaelic congregations or from that of the nineteenth-century Free Church, the popular interest in St Kilda greatly exceeded that in the rest of Gaelic Scotland. What was most striking to the visitors (few of whom had other experiences of Gaelic worship) was the strict Sabbatarianism of the islanders. According to Connell, 'this extraordinary fanaticism' had 'crippled' the fishing industry, or more specifically, his own wish to be taken out in the boat by the islanders.* Dr Fraser MacDonald.[64]

63. Campbell, Ian D., in *The Stornoway Gazette*, 31 August 2000.
64. MacDonald, 'St Kilda and the Sublime', 165.

10. *For the most part the popular accounts posit the islanders as the dupes of modernity, too simple to withstand the seductive advance of religion, education and trade.* Dr Fraser MacDonald.[65]

There can be little doubt that, as Campbell suggests, the church and faith of the St Kildans strengthened their capacity to remain in their community until 1930. The strategically important role of ministers, missionaries and teachers in providing a strong focal point for the St Kildan community is more than apparent in the records for the period after 1900, and it was, of course, the principal reason for the verbal attacks mounted by Sands and Connell before 1900. As in other communities in the Highlands and Islands, the Christian faith created, through shared belief, an additionally cohesive bond, whose power to keep the community together in good times and bad far outweighed any disagreements which it may have caused in the mid-nineteenth century and later. Their church and faith also offered St Kildans an opportunity for self-expression and communal celebration, particularly through singing, in which the community could articulate its own distinctive forms of melody, and, at the same time, be reminded of the wider community of Christian believers beyond its shores, who sang the same Psalms and read the same Bible. The church pulpit provided intellectual stimulation, most notably in Communion Seasons, to the extent that St Kildans were apparently able to challenge their minister when his preaching did not come up to the standard they expected (as also happened in other Hebridean communities).[66] More problematically for any self-righteous and self-satisfied visitors who stepped ashore in their domain, the St Kildans were able

---

65. Ibid., 167
66. Robson, *St Kilda*, 631.

to challenge, and even to pierce, the protective cocoon of their preconceived expectations. As MacDonald argues, it made those visitors feel deeply uncomfortable, especially if they came with a sense of superiority, and had to face the searching sermons of MacKay, which, as Sands discovered to his considerable distaste, MacKay was prepared to translate into English for his sole benefit, thus making him feel potentially 'vulnerable' and 'got at'. Far from being 'fanatics' or 'dupes of modernity', the evidence indicates that the St Kildans, like their minister, were purposefully strong in their beliefs, which they found highly relevant and comforting in their own circumstances, as did similar communities of believers in other parts of the Highlands and Islands. Whether we agree or disagree with their beliefs or their religious conventions is, in the end, of little relevance to the undeniably robust manner in which they embraced both the Christian faith and its practice. Clearly, 'it worked for them'. It is understandable that, in our own deeply secular age, some of us may find their rugged devotion uncomfortable, and that we may seek to find fault with them and with their mentors, in an effort to 'explain it all away'. Like St Kilda itself, however, the record of their faith remains strong and enduring in the midst of the storm.

7. Conclusions

In order to re-evaluate the role of faith and church in St Kilda, and in the day-to-day life of the St Kildans, we must recognise the following:

(a) A great deal of prejudiced and prejudicial writing exists about St Kildan life, and especially its Christian religious dimension. The basis for such an approach was laid in the last quarter of the nineteenth century, from 1875 onwards, when St Kilda suddenly became much more accessible to the outside world, especially through steamship services.

The works of John Sands and Robert Connell set a highly problematic precedent for subsequent (especially post-1960) historians. The emerging picture was made all the more complex by the readiness of these more recent historians to accept their general perceptions of the 'gloom' and 'tyranny' inflicted on the St Kildans by promulgators of the Christian faith. Their accounts, which have played well with those who are broadly 'hostile' to the Christian faith, or to certain expressions of it, were (and still are) usually 'privileged' over accounts provided by writers resident in St Kilda in the period 1900–1930, who were thoroughly familiar with the community under discussion. The contrast between the nineteenth-century accounts and those of the latter group, who were alive in the twentieth century, is stark, to say the least. Those of us who do know the Hebrides and their churches at first hand find it hard to believe that, whatever the quality of individual ministers and their ministries may have been before 1900, the St Kildans' own view of their church and faith would have been much different in the period 1820–1900.

(b) Until the publication of comparatively recent works by Dr Fraser MacDonald, Michael Robson and John Randall, the most serious problem in assessments of church and faith in St Kilda has been the authors' presentation of the St Kildan 'brand' of Christianity as particular to St Kilda. It was not, in fact, *sui generis*. The form and practice of the Christian faith in St Kilda would have been, and indeed are, instantly recognisable to other Gaelic-speaking communities in the Northern Highlands and Hebrides. The Christian faith in the Gaelic areas interacted with the indigenous culture, and produced a distinctive expression of the faith which gave prominence to solemnity, seriousness and Sabbath-keeping.

139

It also fostered an indigenous form of long-line Psalm-singing (with precentor), which, together with the features already noted, has helped to define 'Highland religion'. This expression of the faith has proved highly durable, and has been retained in the face of 'lowlandising' and 'secularising' influences. The visits of the Rev. John MacDonald to St Kilda from 1822 guaranteed that the church and faith in St Kilda would be an integral part of the wider Highland and Hebridean Protestant 'faith group', with its distinguishing features. Most of the criticisms made of the practice of the Christian faith in St Kilda could be made of many other communities in the Scottish Highlands and Islands, and are thus inadmissible as evidence of the 'peculiarity' of St Kilda or of some form of 'religious tyranny' in Hirta. Indeed, some of these same criticisms of the churches (usually the Free Church of Scotland and the Free Presbyterian Church) can be heard of, and in, the Outer Hebrides in the present day.

(c) The post-1960 popular accounts contain a noticeable element of antipathy towards Christianity, which, in its 'missionary' dimension, is seen as a form of imperialism, coming down from the days of 'faith and flag' (as depicted in MacGregor's Gaelic poem above). 'Natives' are portrayed as victims, forced or 'conned' into accepting alien worldviews, which then destroy their way of life. It needs to be noted, however, that post-1960 writers (flourishing in the period of African decolonisation) can *themselves* be 'imperialist', even in their well-intentioned attempts to show the alleged tyranny imposed on or by others. It is deeply thought-provoking and grimly ironic that writers of the mid-1960s could be so securely shackled to outmoded, centralist and imperialist worldviews.

(d) There are various theoretical 'problems' at the heart of the post-1960 works, especially in their evaluation of church and faith in St Kilda. The popular historical accounts (by Steel and MacLean, most obviously) are broadly theory-driven, rather than evidence-driven, and their approach can be matched without any difficulty in the 'evaluations' provided by other writers who deal with South Sea islanders.

(e) The main 1876–1887 writings on St Kilda and also their post-1960 popular successors appear to derive their energy from an ongoing power-struggle, palpable within the texts, in which the 'forces' change with time. The nineteenth-century volumes could be said to depict a contest for 'cultural space', between the Rev. John MacKay, on the one hand, and Sands and Connell on the other. The contest can also be seen as one between the non-St Kildan forces of external secularisation, represented by the new arrivals, and the forces of internal St Kildan religious 'authority', represented by the Rev. John MacKay. More recent writers, who espouse anthropological perspectives on religion, add their own range of contests to the original mix. Anthropologists' views of religion (other than 'natural environment religion' [my phrase]) tend to be inherently hostile, largely because of perceived contests relating to 'power', and the usurping of 'primitive power' by 'modern power' (commonly represented by the dreaded 'missionary'). The most obvious (perceived) dichotomy in the analyses of St Kilda's religious practices offered by 'popular' post-1960 non-St Kildan writers is between the way of life 'previously governed by wind and tide' and that now governed by 'the demands of regular church-going'.

(f) Modern anthropologists, equipped with all the gadgetry and comforts of the present day, and happy to foster even more 'intrusion' into fragile communities, are constantly looking for 'natural man/humanity', at one with nature (Utopia) and thus naturally 'empowered', and not disturbed by external

141

'intrusions' (Dystopia), and thus unnaturally 'disempowered'.
According to Dr Fraser MacDonald, writers of a similar bent
are 'terminally nostalgic' at heart.

(g) Anthropologists and 'popular' historical writers in a
similar mould are not at all worried about the fact that they
themselves are external to the cultures concerned, have
never experienced them at first hand, and are operating 'to
(theoretical) prescription'. They may see such 'detachment' as
a virtue, which allows them some form of 'neutrality', but the
'truth' is more complex.

(h) We need to be much more critical (in the proper sense) of
late nineteenth-century writings about St Kilda, and to
recognise the biases and agendas which they incorporate,
whether by ignorance or by design. We must understand that
the writings of Sands and Connell are extremely complex
literary and personal documents, and that they require to be
assessed as (inter)textual compositions (and 'deconstructed'
accordingly) before their value as 'historical sources' can
even be considered.

(i) It is equally important to bear in mind not only that the
'author' of a 'text' of any kind has the power to create his/her
own reality, but also that a 'text' seemingly produced by a
single named 'author' can, in fact, be a multi-authored volume,
to which even deceased writers can contribute substantial
amounts. 'Popular' writers, like Steel and MacLean, who rely
on tourists' and visitors' accounts of an earlier day, have their
hands 'led at the pen', and can be trapped within the same
'discourse' as their sources, thus (re)producing much the
same kind of 'text'. The main difference is that more recent
work is often validated by certain 'networks'/ 'structures' of
academic thought and discipline, which give it even greater
'power' and authority than its original sources.

(j) A portion of (real!) neutral ground has to be achieved on which to build the 'new analysis' of church and faith in St Kilda. But can it ever be achieved?

(k) We can make progress, first and foremost, by placing the Christian faith and conventions of the St Kildans within wider perspectives relevant to the Hebrides and the Highlands as a whole. The research question that we must now tackle is not, 'How peculiar was St Kilda in and of itself?' It is, 'How did St Kilda fit into, or differ from, the wider patterns of the Highlands and Hebrides?'

(l) Within these wider, but home-based, perspectives, which must be informed by a proper knowledge of the cultural and ecclesiastical region of which St Kilda formed a part, the church and faith of the St Kildans – and much else about St Kilda – may well turn out to be surprisingly 'normal'.

8. …and finally…

Services in the church in St Kilda were resumed briefly when some St Kildans returned in the summer during the 1930s to repair and maintain their former homes. One of the last acts of worship in this context was witnessed by Robert Atkinson, an outstanding writer and photographer, who visited St Kilda in 1938, along with Finlay MacQueen, Neil Gillies and Mrs Gillies. Atkinson writes poignantly:

Finlay in spectacles conducted the service; prayers, psalms read and then sung, Bible reading, a twenty-minute sermon. Finlay read with fearful histrionic emphasis. They all sang the psalms in a soaring and whooping dirge, often nasally out of tune or out of time with each other, but they made a loud unselfconscious noise. The prayers were said fervently in an almost agonised hoarse whisper. Finlay's sermon echoed round the dust-deep room. 'Change and decay in all around I see' ... perhaps.

The large dirty room and the congregation of three – or four – put a strangeness on the performance which the St Kildans evidently did not feel; and why indeed should they? But I was overtaken by the queerness of it; the circumstances bizarre to me of fallen plaster and tattered books were irrelevant to them. They had been reared from birth to this religion so it came as naturally and essentially to them as eating or drinking (though it was a little odd that they didn't clear up their sacred house). For myself, from a southern orthodoxy of ignorance of anything to do with the Church, the oddness was not so much in the circumstances of the service as in the fact that it happened at all.[67]

Atkinson recognised not so much the 'peculiarity' of this deeply meaningful act of worship, but his own inability to comprehend its true significance, stemming from his 'ignorance' of appropriate ecclesiastical and spiritual perspectives. He did not make the egregious and erroneous assumptions or value-judgments that so many of his fellow authors had made, and would continue to make, across more than two hundred years. He thus honoured, rather than demeaned, those post-exilic St Kildans in the island of their birth.

Acknowledgements

Writing the published version of this complex paper took far longer, and was much more challenging, than I could ever have anticipated, and I am most grateful to John Randall of the Islands Book Trust for exercising both patience and mercy

---

67. Atkinson, *Island Going*, 236.

towards the author as he went far beyond his deadline. Given the nature of the paper, I would not wish to implicate anyone in the arguments that I have advanced, but I am most grateful (again) to John Randall for reading earlier drafts and for keeping me on the right track when I was 'prone to wander'. Dr Fraser MacDonald's incisive analysis in *Ecumene* showed me the way, and cleared the path. I owe a further debt to Dr Sheila Kidd, Celtic and Gaelic, University of Glasgow, for providing a scanned copy of the relevant pages of John N. MacLeod's *Memorials of the Rev. Norman MacLeod*. In another context, she also drew my attention to the invaluable Internet Library, which gave me direct access by computer to the principal nineteenth-century writings used in this paper. My debt to, and my great gratitude for, Michael Robson's monumental research is all the more heartfelt in the context of my own struggle to write this one article. My thanks are also due to the Islands Book Trust for their excellent publications about St Kilda. And last but not least, I could not have functioned without David A. Quine's beautifully serene collection of (auto)biographical writings, which show the utmost respect for the *Hiortaich*, whose 'voices' have been a balm to my mind, as well as an inspiration to 'keep going'. *Tapadh leibh uile.*

Bibliography

Ashcroft, Bill, et al., *The Empire Writes Back: Theory and practice in post-colonial literatures*. Routledge, Abingdon, second edn, 2002.

Atkinson, Robert, *Island Going*. William Collins, Glasgow, 1949, and Birlinn, Edinburgh, 2008.

Connell, Robert, *St Kilda and the St Kildians*. Hamilton, Adams & Co., London, and Thomas D. Morison, Glasgow, 1887.

Dòmhnullach, Iain, *Marbhrainn, a rinneadh air Diadhairibh Urramach, Nach Maireann; agus Dàna Spioradail Eile*. John Grant, Edinburgh, 1890.

The Dumbarton Herald. Dumbarton.

Fagan, Brian M., *Clash of Cultures*. AltaMira Press, Walnut Creek, CA, 1998.

Fienup-Riordan, Ann, *Eskimo Essays*. Rutgers University Press, New Brunswick and London, 1990.

Gillies, Donald John, *The Truth about St Kilda: An Islander's Memoir*. Birlinn, Edinburgh, 2010.

Harman, Mary, *An Isle Called Hirte: A History and Culture of St Kilda to 1930*. Maclean Press, Skye, 1997.

Hastings, Adrian (ed.), *A World History of Christianity*. Cassell, London, 1999.

Haswell-Smith, Hamish, *The Scottish Islands*. Canongate Books Ltd., Edinburgh, 2004.

Heathcote, Norman, *St Kilda*. Longmans, London and New York, 1900.

Howells, Richard, *The Myth of the Titanic*. MacMillan Press Ltd, Basingstoke, 1999.

Kearton, Richard, *With Nature and a Camera*. Cassell and Company Ltd, London, Paris, New York and Melbourne, 1898.

Kennedy, John, *The Apostle of the North: The Life and Labours of the Rev. John MacDonald, DD, of Ferintosh*. Free Presbyterian Publications, Glasgow, 1978 repr.

Lawson, Bill, *Croft History: Isle of St Kilda*. Bill Lawson Publications, Harris, 1993.

Lawson, Bill, *St Kilda and its Church: A Hebridean Church in its Historical Setting*. Bill Lawson Publications, Harris, 1993.

Lawson, Bill, et al., *St Kilda: Myth and Reality*. The Islands Book Trust, Lewis, 2007.

MacDonald, Calum, *From Cleits to Castles: A St Kildan Looks Back*. The Islands Book Trust, Lewis, 2010.

MacDonald, Fraser, 'St Kilda and the Sublime', *Ecumene: A Journal of Cultural Geographies*, 8, No. 2, 2001, 151–74.

MacFhearghuis, Calum, *Hiort: Far na laigh a' Ghrian*. Acair, Stornoway, 1995.

Macfie, Alexander L., *Orientalism*. Pearson Education, Harlow, 2002.

MacLean, Charles, *Island on the Edge of the World: Utopian St Kilda and its Passing*. Tom Stacey Ltd, London, 1972. Later reprinted with revision in paperback by Canongate Books Ltd, Edinburgh, 1977.

MacLeod, John N., *Memorials of the Rev. Norman MacLeod*. David Douglas, Edinburgh, 1898.

Meek, Donald E., 'Gaelic Bible, Revival and Mission: the spiritual rebirth of the nineteenth-century Highlands', in *The Church in the Highlands*, ed. James Kirk, 114–45. Scottish Church History Society, Edinburgh, 1998.

Meek, Donald E., *Steamships to St Kilda: John McCallum, Martin Orme, and the Life and Death of an Island Community*. The Islands Book Trust, Lewis, 2010.

Meek, Donald E., *The Scottish Highlands: The Churches and Gaelic Culture*. World Council of Churches, Geneva, 1996.

Meek, Donald E., '"Craobh-sgaoileadh a' Bhìobaill agus an t-Soisgeil:" A Gaelic Song on the Nineteenth-Century Christian Missionary Movement,' in *Fil Súil nGlais: A Grey Eye Looks Back: A Festschrift in honour of Colm Ó Baoill*, ed. Sharon Arbuthnot and Kaarina Hollo. Clann Tuirc, Brig o' Turk, 2007.

Neill, Stephen, *A History of Christian Missions*. The Penguin History of the Church, Vol. 6. Revised edn, Penguin Books, London, 1986.

Pettifer, Julian, and Bradley, Richard, *Missionaries*. BBC Books, London, 1990.

Quine, David A. (ed.), *St Kilda Portraits*. Published by the author, Ambleside, Cumbria, 1988.

Robson, Michael, *St Kilda: Church, Visitors and 'Natives'*. The Islands Book Trust, Lewis, 2005.

Said, Edward W., *Orientalism*. Penguin Books, London, 2003 edn.

Sands, John, *Out of the World, or, Life in St Kilda*. MacLachlan & Stewart, Edinburgh, 1878.

Seton, George, *St Kilda, Past and Present*. William Blackwood and Sons, Edinburgh and London, 1878.

Steel, Tom, *The Life and Death of St Kilda*. National Trust for Scotland, Edinburgh, 1965; expanded and revised edition published by Fontana, London, 1975.

The Stornoway Gazette. Stornoway, Lewis.

The Memoirs of the Rev. Donald John Gillies

John Randall

Introduction

We are looking in this session at two of the very few books about St Kilda written by native St Kildans. We have just heard about the late Calum MacDonald's autobiography. I want now to look at the second book: 'The Truth about St Kilda', based on the memoir of the late Rev. Donald John Gillies, which I edited, and published by Birlinn earlier this year.

Why so few books were written from the inside is one of the main themes of this conference and we will return to this tomorrow.

Today I want to concentrate on what Donald John Gillies has to say on some of the key aspects of living on St Kilda – and contrast this with other perspectives.

Background to the Gillies Manuscript

The Rev. Donald John Gillies was born on St Kilda in 1901 and left the island in 1924 or 1925, emigrating to Canada to pursue his missionary calling in 1927. His manuscript also contains some memories by his elder brother, Neil, who also left the island before the evacuation, but returned regularly during the summers of the years following 1930 to look after the island for the new proprietor, Lord Dumfries.

Details of the ancestry of Neil (1896–1989) and Donald John Gillies (1901–1993) are given in Bill Lawson's 'Croft History – Isle of St Kilda' (1993). They were the sons of John Gillies (1861–1926) and his second wife Ann Ferguson (1865–1952) of Croft No 15 Hiort, situated close to the west end of the village street, at a distance from the church and school.

The Gillieses occupied this croft ever since the new village and crofts were laid out in 1836, replacing the former settlement to the north of the graveyard and the previous run-rig system. Neil and Donald John's great-grandfather, John Gillies, is recorded in the first unofficial census of St Kilda taken by the Rev. John MacDonald of Ferintosh ('The Apostle of the North') in 1822. It would appear that the Gillieses were one of the families from Skye which re-populated St Kilda after an epidemic of small-pox almost wiped out the community in about 1727. On their mother's side, Neil and Donald John were descended from the Fergusons of Crofts Nos 4 and 5 Hiort, whose ancestors moved to St Kilda from Berneray in Harris after 1727.

Through both sides of the family, the brothers were related to individuals who played an important part in the history of St Kilda. One of their great-grandfather's brothers was the colourful and much-travelled Ewen Gillies, who emigrated to Australia in 1852, and then returned to St Kilda to re-marry before emigrating again (to Canada) in 1889. One of their mother's brothers was Neil Ferguson, the St Kilda postmaster, and she was descended from both Donald and Neil Ferguson, elders who had played a prominent part in previous disputes with the Free Church Minister and catechist on the island. So there can be no doubt that Neil and Donald John came from families at the centre of St Kildan life, and are therefore well-placed to give accounts of island life from the inside.

The Manuscript

The manuscript of Donald John Gillies was discovered in Vancouver, Canada, after his death there in 1994. It is written in long-hand in seven notebooks, which were standard school exercise books. There is little attempt to structure the memoirs, just a few section headings but no chapter headings. The text moves in an apparently unplanned way from subject area to subject area, frequently digressing and repeating itself, and shifting erratically from one time period to another. The narrative appears to be interspersed with extracts from newspaper articles from time to time, although these are not clearly identified as different from the author's own observations.

It contains many incomplete sentences, much repetition, and frequent examples of what to a contemporary eye would be regarded as poor construction and composition. It seems at first sight strange that a Minister like the Rev. Donald John Gillies should have such a poor command of written language. It should of course be borne in mind that he was over 80 when he wrote the memoir. Part of the explanation may also be that he is a native Gaelic speaker writing in an acquired language.

But the issue goes deeper than this. It is difficult to escape the conclusion that Donald John Gillies, while no doubt a fluent speaker and preacher, was uncomfortable when attempting to commit his thoughts to paper, whether in Gaelic or English. So even Gaelic words are sometimes recorded phonetically rather than as written. It is perhaps easier to interpret the manuscript as an attempt by someone brought up in an overwhelmingly oral culture to write down his thoughts in an unfamiliar medium.

I want now to examine some of the key aspects of the content of Donald John's memoir, and how what he has to say contrasts with conventional wisdom, often written from the outside.

(1) The Natural World and Environment of St Kilda

A major reason why people have wanted to visit St Kilda in the past, and still do, is its outstanding natural environment, both the dramatic landscape and teeming bird-life. Many books and articles are devoted to this. You will find little of this in the Donald John Gillies memoir. His concerns are about the difficulties of surviving in a harsh and dangerous environment. And his approach to bird-life is rather different from visiting ornithologists.

In his book, there are several descriptions of expeditions in search of birds, for example Manx Shearwater, Puffin, and Gannet. They start off describing the habitats and the need to approach the nesting sites carefully so as not to disturb the birds, very much like an ornithological excursion. Only a little way into the descriptions does it become clear that the purpose of the expedition is to catch and eat the birds!

Nor does Donald John Gillies appear to share the wider research interests of scientists, to whom St Kilda has become a wonderful open-air laboratory – many of the 700+ books and articles about St Kilda are detailed examinations of the flora and fauna, particularly the rare or endemic species such as the St Kildan Wren and St Kildan Field-mouse which have evolved as distinct sub-species because of other populations on the mainland.

I am often struck by a paradox here. The human population were taught and believed for at least 100 years in the literal truth of the Bible, while living in an environment which has become a test-bed for theories of evolution.

I am not pointing up this contrast to say that one group was right and the other wrong – but to illustrate how perceptions can be different when viewed from different perspectives.

(2) Religion and the Christian Culture of St Kilda

Which brings us to the controversial subject of religion and the role of the Church in St Kilda, which has already been examined so expertly by Donald Meek.

What stands out from Donald John's account is the overwhelming importance and pervasiveness of religion to life on St Kilda. Even allowing for the fact that Donald John Gillies became a Minister, there is no doubt from his account that Presbyterian religion, and the view of the world which it embodied, played a central part in St Kildan life. From the very first pages of the narrative to the last, it is made clear that the purpose of life, and the values which are to be treasured and upheld, derive from Christianity and the teachings of the Bible.

Donald John's mother only read religious books and had an unwavering faith in the truth of the Bible. Donald John's father, like other prominent members of the community, had a deep knowledge of the Bible. The standing of men depended to a considerable extent on their ability to quote from and interpret the Bible, for example on *La Ceist* at the communions. A large number of the stories told by the St Kildans seem to have been derived from the Bible, or have biblical allusions.

And there is no suggestion that this was in any sense a dogma forced on the people by dominant Ministers or elders, as some of the popular caricatures of St Kildan life would suggest. On the contrary, religion was the vital integrating force of community life, apparently accepted and wholeheartedly endorsed by the great majority of St Kildans. Christianity was at the heart of their culture. Family worship was central to daily life. Sundays were observed universally and unquestioningly as the Lord's Day. The values of humility, love, and kindness, and the need for salvation, were celebrated and accepted.

In all of this, it is doubtful whether St Kildans were so different from many other rural Gaelic-speaking communities at the time in the Presbyterian parts of the Outer Hebrides. Outside observers, many of whom had never visited other places in the Hebrides, saw St Kilda as a place apart when in many ways its customs and beliefs were typical of a much wider area. I will return to this theme.

(3) Traditions

The manuscript sheds invaluable light on many regular customs and beliefs. For example, the periodic excursions of men to Boreray to see to the sheep and cut peats is outlined in a matter-of-fact and unsentimental way which adds to our understanding of the economic functions which Boreray (and also Soay and Dun) played in St Kildan life. The various underground dwellings on Boreray, each belonging to a particular family, are described, along with the system of sending messages from Boreray to Hirta involving the cutting of turf patches at particular spots on Boreray visible from the main island.

And the role of the St Kildan Parliament, sensationalised and exaggerated by the journalist John Sands in the 1870s, is clarified. It did not meet on a daily basis, and its key role during Donald John's childhood was to decide on the allocation of birds and bird-cliffs between the various families on the island. Like the role of the Church, one doubts whether the Parliament was so different from gatherings in many other islands or rural areas where communal activity of one sort or another was vital to the economic functioning of the community.

(4) The Evacuation

A further fascinating and important point is Donald John's analysis of the reasons for St Kilda's decline and eventual abandonment. In his view, and those of other St Kildans whom he spoke to after the evacuation in 1930, the basic reason was lack of manpower to carry out community tasks, a gradually worsening predicament which he traces to the impact of the First World War. The stationing of military forces and installations on the island during the First World War led to a greater understanding by many of the younger generation of St Kildans of the perceived benefits of life outside the island. Once a few families and younger people emigrated, it became progressively more difficult for the community to sustain itself.

Again, this is not a unique phenomenon. Many other islands in the Outer Hebrides have become uninhabited in the 19th and 20th centuries under the influence of much the same economic and social pressures.

Nor was this decline and eventual evacuation seen by most of the St Kildans as a source of regret. There was inevitably and understandably a nostalgia for the old days, and certainly a feeling that many valuable things had been lost. But it is striking that all those St Kildans interviewed by Donald John and his brother on the mainland following the evacuation were of the view that the move had been inevitable and indeed on balance beneficial. Apart from criticism that the Government had failed for many years to supply a postal service to the island, there seems to have been no resentment at the community's treatment by the authorities – indeed at several points Donald John is at pains to emphasise how well the St Kildans were treated both before and at the time of the evacuation.

Conclusion

As a tail-piece, I sometimes think that one of the main benefits of all the incredible amount of writing about St Kilda is the insight it gives us into the history of much of the Western Isles more generally. Indeed, the more I look at the history of St Kilda, the more I am struck by how much it had in common with other Hebridean islands – contrary to the myth that St Kilda was a world apart. It did after all share most of the key developments in the history of many larger islands such as Lewis, Harris, and Skye – prehistoric settlement, important Norse influence, an overwhelmingly Gaelic language and culture for many centuries, and the later influence of an evangelical Presbyterian religion. But many of the visitors who swarmed to St Kilda in the 19th century had never been to other islands, and described things which they thought were unique – frequent and long religious services on Sunday, for example – but which actually were typical of the wider Gaelic Presbyterian culture of which St Kilda was part.

And the issue of outside views from a dominant culture setting an agenda which is not necessarily shared by islanders themselves has not gone away. I doubt if the way the islands are widely seen by incoming families, tourists and outside commentators today as predominantly a place of peace and quiet, or an unspoilt environment which must be protected from development, is one which is widely shared by local people. And there are plenty of mainland-based journalists – and others – who still like nothing better than to run stories about the 'Wee Frees', their repressive and out-moded regime, and the alleged damage this is doing to the economic and social life of the islands. It makes a good story, just as did the writings of the journalist John Sands in the 1870s, who invented the myths of the St Kilda Parliament and the St Kilda mail-boat.

So, to sum up, I believe the voluminous accounts of St Kilda by visitors and journalists do have a value. But, paradoxically, it is because they give us an insight into a society which was in many respects not unique, but shared many characteristics with other parts of the Hebrides which never got the same attention. They also provide a stark warning of how the culture of the Outer Hebrides is still under threat today.

The title of Donald John's book is 'The Truth about St Kilda' – not a title I chose! 'Truth' is a multi-faceted concept and, as with any community, it is impossible for any written account to encompass all aspects of the truth of life on St Kilda. But as we search for the 'truth', it is surely important to pay particular attention to the views of people like Donald John Gillies and his brother, who actually lived in the island as part of the St Kildan community for many years.

While it cannot be ruled out that the Gillieses may have been repeating views about the island which were derived from other writers, or others they had met from outside the island, it is reasonable to suppose that on central issues such as religion and attitudes towards the evacuation, they are reflecting the beliefs and assumptions of the community. What they have to say may not be well written, or support the romantic, fashionable, or critical views of outside observers, but on many topics it is likely to be authentic and so worthy of respect by those who are seeking 'the truth'.

A History of Photography in St Kilda

Martin Padget

Since its invention in the mid nineteenth century, photography has become one of the most popular and significant ways of recording and making sense of the world about us. This is particularly true of a location such as St Kilda, where the use of the camera has proved instrumental in shaping perceptions of the dramatic topography of the archipelago, its abundant wildlife and its iconic human community. We have only to think of G.W. Wilson & Co.'s celebrated portrait of the St Kilda Parliament from 1886, the myriad historical views of the distinctively curved line of cottages along Hirta's Main Street in both their inhabited and ruined state, and more contemporary aerial shots of the archipelago to gain an apt sense of the visual impact of St Kilda. In the following pages I will provide a brief history of photography in St Kilda that points out the various ways in which the archipelago has been represented through the camera lens and assess the motivation of the various photographers concerned. Its chronology runs from 1860, when the first known photographs of islanders were created by Captain F. W. L. Thomas, to 1938, when Robert Atkinson visited Hirta eight years after the evacuation of the community. In other words, I have narrowed the chronological range of the discussion to the period in which an indigenous culture of Gaelic-speaking islanders inhabited Hirta.[1]

Captain Frederick William Leopold Thomas (1817–85) created the first photographs of St Kilda when he visited Hirta on board *HMS Porcupine* during his employment with the Scottish hydrographical survey in 1860. Initially photography was the preserve of gentleman amateurs, such as the Englishman William Henry Fox Talbot, who invented the calotype (a paper-based negative process) in 1841 and photographed locations associated with Sir Walter Scott's life and works for one of the earliest photographic books, *Sun Pictures in Scotland* (1845). By the year of Thomas' visit to St Kilda, the London Stereoscopic Company could boast of a stock of over one hundred thousand photographs that were consumed avidly by a clientele of middle-class Britons.[2] As the company's name suggests, these stereo images were printed in pairs that were mounted on stiff cardboard mounts and then viewed through binocular viewers that provided the illusion of three-dimensional imagery. Victorians also purchased myriad cartes-de-visite, small size images that typically represented family members as well as of notable members of society, and larger format prints of locations throughout the British Isles and the wider world. By the close of the nineteenth century, the range of photographic formats had increased to include magic lantern slides, illustrations in books and journals (using the half-tone process), and postcards. The extent and range of photographic

---

1. For discussions of photography and visual representation of St Kilda and the Western Isles, see Ian Spring, 'Land of Lost Dreams – Representing St Kilda', *Cultural Studies* 4, no. 2 (May 1990): 156–75; Fraser MacDonald, 'St. Kilda and the Sublime', *Cultural Geographies*, Vol. 8, No. 2 (2001): 151–74; and Martin Padget, *Photographers of the Western Isles* (Edinburgh: John Donald, 2010), chapters two and five.

2. John Jones, *Wonders of the Stereoscope* (London: Jonathan Cape, 1976), 16.

imagery available to the public was astonishing considering the relative dearth of commonly available illustrations of landscapes and communities earlier in the century.[3]

Thomas is a fascinating figure whose passionate interest in antiquarian research contributed greatly to the Victorian-era understanding of the ancient and historical monuments of Scotland. During the course of his work with the hydrographical survey of the coastal waters around the Western Isles, Thomas had ample opportunity to conduct his antiquarian investigations. He contributed many papers to antiquarian journals and served as vice president of the Society of Antiquaries of Scotland in Edinburgh.[4] Having joined the Photographic Society of Scotland in 1856, Thomas purchased a stereoscopic camera and created a series of photographs that illustrated his travels through the Western Isles during the late 1850s and 1860s.[5] He mounted these images, which include twenty-one photographs of St Kilda, in an album that is now held by the National Archives of Scotland.[6] All but two of the St Kilda images are portraits, which show islanders in various groupings and as individuals. Not all of the portraits are of native St Kildans, however, for Thomas also photographed

3. For useful general histories of photography, see Michel Frizot, ed., *The New History of Photography* (Köln: Könemann, 1998), Mary Warner Marien, *Photography: A Cultural History* (London: Laurence King Publishing, 2002), and Naomi Rosenblum, *A World History of Photography* (New York: Abbeville Press, 1989).

4. For a good example of Thomas' antiquarian publications, see Captain F. W. L. Thomas, 'On the Primitive Dwellings and Hypogea of the Outer Hebrides', *Proceedings of the Society of Antiquaries of Scotland*, vol. 7 (1866): 153–95.

5. Information drawn from the EdinPhoto website – http://www.edinphoto.org.uk/3/3_pss_members_thomas.htm.

6. Captain F. W. L. Thomas, *Album of Photographs, Woodcuts and Lithographs* (1857–c.1870); GD492/12, National Archives of Scotland, Edinburgh.

Duncan Kennedy, the resident Free Church catechist, Norman McRaild, the factor for St Kilda, and a stonemason named Campbell who was in temporary residence at the time of the visit.

Similar to all the other portraits, Thomas' photograph of three St Kilda boys (Figure 1) was made in the doorway to the manse, where Kennedy resided. This location was chosen because subjects were more likely to remain still when leaning against

Figure 1. Captain F. W. L. Thomas, Bonnie Barnies *(1860).*
Reproduced with the permission of the WS Society, Edinburgh

161

a firm structure during the long exposures that were required in early photography. In this case, whilst the boys do not appear to be leaning against the doorframe, the careful placement of their arms indicates another means for photographers of the day to prevent the movement of their subjects. The intimate arrangement of the boys also conveys a rather sentimental image of the boys that was in keeping with Victorian-era ideas of childhood character.[7] Even though the arrangement of the boys was almost certainly orchestrated by Thomas as he prepared to photograph them, the portrait also suggests something of the great emotional investment that the St Kilda population placed in children who survived the exceptionally high infant mortality rate that prevailed throughout most of the eighteenth and nineteenth centuries. A quarter century after Thomas created this photograph, the journalist Robert Connell observed that new born children were wrapped in flannel after birth rather than given their own clothes: 'It is a melancholy testimony to [lockjaw's] ravages and to the ghastly dread with which it fills the people's minds that even still a mother never thinks of providing clothing for her babe until she sees whether or not it survives the first crucial days.'[8] The cause of the infants' deaths was tetanus infection, which most probably was communicated through the midwife not sterilising the knife used to cut the umbilical cord at birth.[9] From the 1890s onward, when the resident missionary,

7. For a discussion of the representation of children in Victorian photography, see Lindsay Smith, *The Politics of Focus: Women, Children and Nineteenth-Century Photography* (Manchester: Manchester University Press, 1998).

8. Robert Connell, *St. Kilda and the St. Kildians* (London: Hamilton, Adams and Co.; Glasgow: Thomas D. Morison, 1887), 110.

9. P. Stride, 'St. Kilda, the Neonatal Tetanus Tragedy of the Nineteenth Century and Some Twenty-First Century Answers,' *The Journal of the Royal College of Physicians of Edinburgh* 38 (2008): 70–77.

the Reverend Angus Giddes, was provided medical training on the mainland, the impact of tetanus infection was considerably lessened.[10]

How did the islanders respond to being photographed on the first occasion a camera was taken into their midst? In his book *St Kilda: Past and Present* (1878), George Seton provides an answer to this question:

> When the 'Porcupine' touched at St Kilda in 1860, several of the islanders went on board to see the wonders of the vessel; and when they appeared somewhat reluctant to go ashore, it turned out, upon inquiry, that they expected to be remunerated for their trouble! Some of them seriously expected that Captain Thomas would pay them for having allowed him to take their photographs. Whether this arose from selfishness or simplicity, may perhaps be somewhat open to question, although probably the Nairn mason employed by Captain Otter to construct a landing-place would have had very little doubt about the subject—his estimate of the St. Kildans being that they were 'the most knowingist people he had ever come across!'[11]

It may seem extraordinary that the islanders would have sought payment for allowing themselves to be photographed on the very first occasion that a camera was taken to Hirta. In fact, this request was consistent with their previously articulated desire to

10.   For discussions of the prevalence of infantile tetanus, see Charles Maclean, *Island on the Edge of the World: The Story of St. Kilda* (rev. ed.; Edinburgh: Canongate, 2006), 133–35; and Tom Steel, *The Life and Death of St. Kilda* (London: Collins, 1975): 100–5. The condition was widely noted by travellers to Hirta, particularly during the second half of the nineteenth century.

11.   George Seton, *St. Kilda: Past and Present* (Edinburgh and London: William Blackwood and Sons, 1878), 255.

exchange goods and money provided by visitors, other than the proprietor's factor, for displays of fowling. Vivid descriptions of the St Kilda men's fowling skills feature in two classic accounts of travel to Hirta, Martin Martin's *A Late Voyage to St Kilda* (1697) and Kenneth Macaulay's *The History of St Kilda* (1764), but it was not until the nineteenth century that remuneration was sought for such displays. During the 1830s, two steam-powered vessels, first the *Glenalbyn* in 1834 and then the *Vulcan* in 1838, anchored in Village Bay before their tourist passengers were rowed to shore.[12] It was in the aftermath of these and further visits by yacht that Neil MacKenzie, the resident minister in the years leading up to the Disruption of 1843, remarked on the ways in which the St Kildans played up to the expectations of visitors by exaggerating their own primitivism:

> *Encouraged by the amazing credulity of the ordinary tourist, the natives have got to be very successful in imposing upon them. The tourist comes with a certain idea in his mind as to what the native is like, and would be disappointed if they did not find him like that; this the natives have been shrewd enough to discover and turn to their own profit. For example, when they went on board a yacht they would pretend that they thought all the polished brass was gold, and the owner must be enormously wealthy. Yet, when in a few minutes after they might be offered the choice of several coins, selecting not the gold but the largest as if they had no idea of the relative value of the different metals. ... [A]ll the time they would be saying to themselves in Gaelic, 'if we*

---

12.   For a detailed account of the period in which the first steamers arrived at St Kilda, see Michael Robson, *St Kilda: Church, Visitors and 'Natives'* (Port of Ness: The Islands Book Trust, 2006), 337–51.

*seem to be paying great attention and make them believe
that we are simple, they will be sure before they go away to
give us something much better.*[13]

Mackenzie's words help us appreciate the degree to which
St Kildans quickly became accustomed to dealing with the
demands and exploiting the desires of leisure travellers during
the decades leading up to the introduction of regular steamer
travel to Hirta in 1877. In due course it became common for
visitors to publish accounts of travel to St Kilda in newspapers
and journals of the day. One such visitor was Edward Bradbury,
whose illuminating article 'From St Pancras to St Kilda'
appeared in the periodical *London Society* in 1884. As the title
suggests, Bradbury began his journey in London, travelling on
board the Midland Pullman sleeper train to St Enoch's Station
in Glasgow, where his party spent the night at the station hotel
before proceeding by steamer to Hirta. He records the train
'thundering through the sleeping counties at fifty miles an hour',
an image of high speed and advanced industrial technology
that contrasts markedly with the isolation and slow pace of
life at St Kilda, which Bradbury notes lies 'outside the steerage
course of vessels'.[14] Similar to many other authors of accounts
of travel to the archipelago during the late nineteenth and early
twentieth centuries, Bradbury emphasised the remoteness of
the St Kildans even as he anticipated the day when Hirta would
draw a substantially higher number of visitors: 'As St Kilda and
the romantic voyage to the island become better known, it will,
no doubt, be recognised as a new holiday ground for the British

---

13.   Quoted in Andrew Fleming, *St. Kilda and the Wider World:
Tales of an Iconic Island* (Macclesfield: Windgather Press, 2005), 8–9.
14.   Edward Bradbury, 'From St Pancras to St Kilda', *London Society:
An Illustrated Magazine of Light and Amusing Literature for the Hours of
Relaxation*, Vol. 46, No. 274 (October 1884): 461 (459–68).

tourist, and with this invasion the place will lose some of its novelty, and the inhabitants their unaffected simplicity.'[15]

The camera played a significant role in documenting the invasion of which Bradbury spoke, and was itself representative of the outside forces that he thought would undermine the moral character of the St Kildans. David Whyte, an Inverness-based professional photographer, provided a telling example of this dual role when he visited the archipelago in June 1884. He depicted a vibrant scene of encounter between island hosts, their minister and a party of visitors, including the crewmembers of at least one vessel (Figure 2). The photograph shows people clustered about the Reverend John MacKay, the resident Free Church minister between 1865 and 1889, who holds a monkey in the middle of the frame. From a purely visual point of view, this is a fascinating image for its documentation of the intermingling of islanders and visitors in a scenario that played out again and again as increasing numbers of visitors were drawn to Hirta. Notably the photograph features only older members of the community, for at the time of Whyte's visit two-thirds of the population were away grazing cattle at Gleann Mòr in the northwest of Hirta. The photograph accrues added significance when we note its accompanying caption in the album in which it was collected. This caption reads: 'The Minister and the Monkey. The former wears a tall hat to distinguish him.'[16] This rather derogatory comment subscribed to the negative view of Mackay that prevailed among many visitors after the publication of the second edition of John Sands' book *Out of the World; or, Life in St Kilda* in 1878. Sands, who made two extended visits to St Kilda in 1875 and 1876, fell out with the minister and caricatured him mercilessly in an illustration that appears in *Out of the World*.[17]

15.   Bradbury, 'From St Pancras to St Kilda', 462.

16.   Henry Evans, *St Kilda, 1884*, n.p.

17.   For discussion of Sands' impact on the island community, see Robson, *St Kilda*, part vi, passim.

Figure 2. David Whyte, The Minister and the Monkey (1884).
Reproduced by permission of David Wilson

The close engagement of St Kildans and visitors on board steamers and yachts caused Mackay to be concerned about the impact of tourism on the community. When the Napier Commission visited Hirta in 1883 during its government-appointed inquiry into the conditions in which crofters and landless cottars lived throughout the Highlands and islands, Mackay commented on various aspects of life on St Kilda. He noted that when steamers arrived, visitors tended to leave '*a good deal of money among the people*'. In general he was not impressed by tourists' behaviour, stating they were 'annoying' when they remained on the island over the Sabbath and observing of some: '*They go about the hills, and go seeing through the windows and striking the dogs and one thing and another.*'[18] In the light of these comments, we might well wonder if Mackay sensed that he might be held up as an object of ridicule when he was encouraged by a visitor, perhaps a member of Whyte's party, to hold the monkey.

During his trip to St Kilda, Whyte made an impressive number of photographs of the archipelago. He was commissioned to do so by Henry Evans, owner of the steam yacht on which he voyaged from Oban, and Alexander Ross, an architect, keen amateur geologist and fellow resident of Inverness.[19] From his negatives Whyte created a set of prints, which Evans mounted in a black leather bound album on which the gilt inlaid title *St Kilda, 1884* appears. This album, which remains in private hands, was for many years owned by the renowned naturalist and author, Sir Frank Fraser Darling. It contains almost forty original photographs, primarily topographical views that were

18. *Report of Her Majesty's Commissioners of Inquiry into the Condition of the Crofters and Cottars in the Highlands and Islands of Scotland, with Appendices*, British Parliamentary Papers (Agriculture) 21–5 (Shannon: Irish University Press, 1969), 865–66.
19. For an account of the trip, see Alexander Ross, 'A Visit to St. Kilda', *Transactions of the Inverness Scientific Society* 3 (1883–88): 72–91.

designed to show the relief and geological character of the various islands and stacks in the archipelago. Whyte also created a set of lantern slides, which were used by Ross to illustrate a lecture on the geological history of St Kilda to members of the Inverness Scientific Society. The overall purpose of the expedition was scientific, and clearly the novelty of Whyte's photograph of Mackay holding a monkey was the exception rather than the rule in this seriously minded undertaking.

Two years after Whyte departed Hirta, a second professional photographer made his way to St Kilda. Norman Macleod worked for G.W. Wilson & Co., one of the most successful and influential photographic companies of the Victorian period, which had developed a worldwide reach by the 1880s from its base in Aberdeen.[20] In fact Macleod travelled through the Highlands with his employer, George Washington Wilson, during the summer of 1886. Wilson, who was now in his early sixties and beginning to experience the ill health that would blight his final years, was one of Scotland's foremost photographers of landscapes, architectural views and cityscapes. Quite early in his career, Wilson photographed extensively in Skye, Staffa and Iona, after these locations became firmly established on routes of popular travel through the west Highlands and Inner Hebrides. However he did not arrange for St Kilda to be photographed until a market for images of this location developed during the 1880s. Macleod's photographs were initially distributed in the form of black and white prints and hand-coloured lantern slides. Later they were also made available as postcards. After a post office was

20. See Roger Taylor, *George Washington Wilson: Artist and Photographer, 1823–93* (Aberdeen: Aberdeen University Press, 1981); and Alastair Durie, 'Tourism and Commercial Photography in Victorian Scotland: The Rise and Fall of G.W. Wilson & Co., 1853–1908,' *Northern Scotland* 12 (1992): 89–104.

established on Hirta in the early 1900s, visitors were keen to send franked postcards from the island. During 1907–08, over 1,400 cards were sent from St Kilda to addresses across the globe.[21]

Among the photographs that Macleod created during his trip is an iconic portrait of the St Kilda Parliament (Figure 3). Thirteen men stand on either side of Main Street, half their number barefoot and all wearing homespun tweed clothing and bonnets to the head. Smoke rises atmospherically from cottage chimneys in the background, while several dogs mingle along the stone-edged pathway. Standing half-relaxed with hands in their pockets, the men appear to be self-possessed in the presence of the camera. On viewing this image, we should try to imagine how on being projected onto a screen in a lecture theatre, the scale and colour of the portrait must truly have captivated late-Victorian audiences. The display of lantern slides freed photography from the constraints of the size of the print, which was limited to the size of the negative until the development of reliable enlargers in the early twentieth century.

Richard and Cherry Kearton visited St Kilda for two weeks in June 1896, arriving on board the steamer *Dunara Castle* and carrying canned food for themselves and gifts of sweets and tobacco for the islanders.[22] Richard, the elder brother who had moved from a humble farming background in the Yorkshire Dales to London to pursue a career at Cassell, the major publishing company, became a well-known author and lecturer on ornithology and related subjects. After pursuing an interest in photography at an early age, Cherry developed into a skilled

---

21.   Steel, *The Life and Death of St. Kilda*, 128.
22.   For an account of this trip, see Richard and Cherry Kearton, *With Nature and a Camera: Being the Adentures and Observations of a Field Naturalist and an Animal Photographer* (London: Cassell, 1897), chapters one and two.

Figure 3. George Washington Wilson, St Kilda Parliament
(1886). Reproduced by permission of Mark Butterworth

photographer of the natural scene. The brothers collaborated
on a number of books of natural history, beginning with *Birds'
Nests, Eggs and Egg-Collecting* (1890), for which Richard supplied
the text and Cherry the images. Their book *With Nature and a
Camera* (1897) includes two chapters recounting their adventures
on St Kilda and features 180 photographs in the form of half-tone
reproductions. Its front cover shows the figure of a photographer
descending a cliff, legs almost at ninety degrees to the sheer
wall of rock, with large tripod strapped to his back. This image
accurately reflects Cherry's willingness to put himself in physical
danger while pursuing ornithological and animal photography.
During their stay, the Kearton brothers participated in a fowling
expedition to Boreray, four miles by rowing boat from Hirta.

171

Figure 4. Cherry Kearton, At the Foot of the Cliffs, Borrera *(1896)*

Cherry photographed a group of twelve men gathered at the foot of Boreray's steep cliffs after descending an 'awful path' (Figure 4).[23] The ten islanders, including the distinctive and frequently photographed figure of Finlay MacQueen on the far right, were joined by Alex Ferguson, a native St Kildan who worked as a successful tweed merchant in Glasgow and is fifth from the left in the image. Richard Kearton sits fourth from the right, looking directly at the camera and perhaps feeling a little anxious at the prospect of the further challenge of leaving the island for the return trip to Hirta. He recollected that '[a]*fter some difficulty and danger, we managed to half-leap and half-tumble into the frail old boat'*, which just two weeks later was broken up on the rocks during a gale.[24]

23.   Kearton, *With Nature and a Camera*, 89.
24.   Kearton, *With Nature and a Camera*, 88.

It is difficult to say for sure how many photographs were made of St Kilda between 1860 and the evacuation of the community in 1930. It seems that relatively few cameras were taken to Hirta until the 1890s, when portable Kodak cameras loaded with celluloid film were introduced to the marketplace. The bulky view cameras and tripods employed by David Whyte and Norman Macleod were used in conjunction with heavy glass plates to produce large negatives that yielded finely detailed prints. The keen amateurs who invested in equipment similar to that which the professionals utilised required not only a good level of income to fund their interest but also a thorough commitment to dealing with the technical challenges involved in mastering the medium. The development of portable and easy-to-use cameras, such as the Pocket Kodak and the Brownie, made it much easier for people in general to create a photographic record of their own experiences. The photographs made by visitors to St Kilda who carried such cameras may number into the thousands. Typically such images would have been kept as mementos of travel and pasted into albums and displayed in picture frames in their owners' homes. Perhaps many such albums and individual prints remain among the succeeding generations of the people who created them. Equally it must be assumed that over the years many photographs, which today would be treasured by libraries, museums and private collectors, have been casually discarded by the owners' relatives and executors, who were not aware of their historical value.

The images made by Michael Stevenson during a trip to St Kilda in 1912 on board the steamer *Hebrides* are an example of photography as pursued by a typical tourist during a four or five hour visit during the Edwardian period. Using a Kodak or similar portable camera, Stevenson, who was employed as a civil engineer, made a series of shots that he collected in a private album, entitled *Photographs Mainly of St. Kilda and Its Inhabitants*, which has been donated to the National Archives of Scotland.[25] Alternately candid and posed, these photographs provide valuable insight into the ways in which islanders and tourists interacted thirty-five years after the introduction of regular steamer travel. Stevenson's photograph *Natives Aboard the 'Hebrides'* (Figure 5) could have been created at the outset or the conclusion of his visit to Hirta. The image shows two young women on board the *Hebrides* carrying pairs of knitted gloves for sale. The women look directly at the camera and clearly have complied with Stevenson's request to be photographed, perhaps so after he offered them a small fee or promised to purchase their wares.

How we interpret the meaning of Stevenson's photographs is dependent on how we make sense of the larger story of St Kilda. For Tom Steel, author of the most popular and influential history of St Kilda, the inexorable decline of the community was due to the islanders' fatal embrace of modernity. In his view, the more that St Kildans communicated and traded with tourists, fishermen, whalers and other outside figures, the more they became dependent on external sources of income and support for their welfare. Of tourism, Steel writes: '*The influx of tourists undermined the economy of the island. Their money led to a decline in productivity and in the people's interest in the traditional way of life on Hirta.*'[26] This idea that the St Kilda community came to lack viability because of its fatal embrace of modern culture has been particularly hard to shake in the popular imagination. I believe this interpretation is simplistic and that it takes away agency from St Kildans as they sought to negotiate the grounds on which they related to various aspects of modern life. The very presence of the two young women in Stevenson's photograph

25.   Michael Stevenson, *Photographs Mainly of St Kilda and Its Inhabitants* (c.1912), National Archives of Scotland, GD1/713/1/13.
26.   Steel, *The Life and Death of St. Kilda*, 135.

St Kildans indicates that they were not passive recipients of tourist interest in their livelihoods but participated in a process of mutual engagement in which they were active, although not necessarily equal partners. Tourism and photography did play a key role in the process by which St Kilda came to be abandoned

Figure 5. Michael Stevenson, Natives Aboard the 'Hebrides' *(c. 1912). Reproduced by permission of SCOTLANDIMAGES. COM, National Archives of Scotland, AAA 02921*

by a growing a proportion of the population in the years leading up to its evacuation in 1930. However the degree to which the 'death' of the St Kilda community should be viewed as the inevitable conclusion to the processes of social and economic change that brought an end to a way of life that Charles Maclean, in another influential study, regards as having '*more in common with a tribe of African bushmen than with the inhabitants of their own capital cities of Edinburgh and London*' is debatable.[27] Recent assessments of St Kilda history, by the archaeologist and historian Andrew Fleming and the cultural geographer Fraser MacDonald, have contested the tragic interpretation of St Kilda's human history by calling into question the degree to which islanders were geographically and culturally isolated from fellow members of the Gàidhealtachd. Fleming, author of the most recent general history of St Kilda, argues that the archipelago was more closely allied to the mainland between the 1600s and twentieth century than has been suggested by Steel. Meanwhile MacDonald contends that it was the St Kildans' very decision to join the Free Church in the aftermath of the Disruption of 1843 that made them far more modern than many visitors realised.[28]

By early 1930 it had become clear that the St Kilda community was no longer viable, and on 29 August that year the remaining thirty-six inhabitants departed their island home for new lives on the mainland. Eight years later, Robert Atkinson travelled to Hirta on board the steamer *Dunara Castle*, which continued to take tourists to Hirta during the summer months. Earlier in the decade, Atkinson, a keen ornithologist who was free to spend

---

27. Charles Maclean, *Island on the Edge of the World: The Story of St Kilda* (Edinburgh: Canongate, 1996), 161.

28. See Andrew Fleming, *St. Kilda and the Wider World: Tales of an Iconic Island* (Macclesfield: Windgather Press, 2005); and MacDonald, 'St. Kilda and the Sublime', 151–74.

vacations away from undergraduate tutors at Oxford University, had contracted island fever, a condition that could only be relieved by visiting remote islands off the west of Scotland. For several years he avoided visiting St Kilda, precisely because the archipelago had become part of the beaten track of travel. Then he reconsidered, rationalising: '*No doubt the romantic interest was well founded. It would be new to see the tourist trade so far-flung, documentary to note picture postcards of the desert island and orange peel in the crumbling village? ... Having got amongst the Western Isles, absurd not to have St Kilda in one's repertoire!*' After the *Dunara Castle* arrived in Village Bay and deposited passengers for their tour of Hirta, Atkinson anticipated the vessel's departure: '*I felt that nothing began until she had gone.*'[29]

What was it that would begin once the steamship and its cargo of tourists departed? For Atkinson the latter represented the intrusion of the outside world into his island idyll. In order to justify his own presence on the island he had to differentiate himself from tourists by virtue of the rationale of his own travels. There was a veneer of scientific purpose to his visit as he set about trapping, measuring and photographing the island's two unique sub-species of mice, the field mouse (*Apodemus sylvaticus hirtensis*) and the house mouse (*Mus musculus muralis*). He also created hides within and outside two cleits in order to photograph another unique species, the St Kilda wren (*Troglodytes troglodytes hirtensis*), sitting on the nest and feeding its young. Atkinson's repeated references to the Kearton brothers' visit over forty years before indicate that he wished to replicate much of what they had done while visiting Hirta. He too walked all over the island and was fascinated by the rich birdlife; investigated the island's cleits, cottages and ruined black houses; and freely interacted with islanders while residing in the factor's house. But unlike Richard

---

29.   Robert Atkinson, *Island Going* (Edinburgh: Birlinn, 1995), 194, 223.

and Cherry Kearton, Atkinson found only a remnant of the St Kilda population in residence, Ann Gillies, her son Neil, and Finlay MacQueen having returned to the island for the summer. Atkinson created an album of photographs that illustrate his various journeys through the Western Isles, and from which he drew when he illustrated his subsequent book *Island Going* (1949).[30] On two of its pages are separate clusters of images that depict Ann Gillies at the spinning wheel and Finlay MacQueen snaring puffins. These must number amongst the last of the many photographs that were taken of each individual during the course of their lifetime on Hirta. The two St Kilda elders are portrayed in sequential images that echo the photographs created by the Kearton brothers forty years before. Atkinson writes of MacQueen: '*Of course he remembered the Keartons, he'd taken them fowling, one of them had a game leg. And when he went on one of his fowling expeditions now, I took the same sort of photographs as Cherry Kearton had taken of him in the days of his prime.*'[31]

A palpable sense of loss underpins Atkinson's account of his three-week stay on Hirta. He arrived too late to see the community properly in action yet close enough time to the island's evacuation to imagine the St Kildans as the Kearton brothers saw them. He searched through dilapidated cottages in which the traces of human habitation were mouldering and rusting away, peered into the dark interiors of byres rank with weeds, and looked about the scene of worship and learning: '*There was a queer stationary quality about schoolroom and church: silence; still air and deep dust; time arrested.*'[32] There is a sense in

---

30.   Atkinson's extensive collection of photography of the Western Isles is now housed in the photographic archive of the School of Scottish Studies, Edinburgh University.

31.   Atkinson, *Island Going*, 259.

32.   Atkinson, *Island Going*, 232.

which twenty-first century visitors to St Kilda are also haunted by a sense of belatedness. We too are compelled to pay homage to a stunning location that was once home to a living community that has captured our imaginations. And we too feel compelled to try capturing the essence of this place through the photographs we take. Whereas previous generations of visitors created glass and celluloid negatives and viewed prints, stereos and lantern slides, today we store images as digital files and view them by way of computers and high definition television screens.

Some Additional Notes on the Lantern Slides of St Kilda

Mark Butterworth

The George Washington Wilson (GWW) series of lantern slides of St Kilda[1] consists of 10 images. Each of them is a superb photograph, taken by Norman Macleod in 1886. The series of lantern slides used in my presentation at the 'Historiography of St Kilda Conference' were all 3¼ inches square, the size in common use in the UK in the late 1880s. However, interest in the images extended beyond the UK. In my collection of GWW slides I have two examples from the sequence in a different format. These slides (Figures 1 and 7) measure 3¼ inches by 4 inches, the standard USA format that time. In my collecting experience and through contact with US collectors of lantern slides it is apparent that any GWW slides for the American market are rarer than the slides for the UK market, making these St Kilda examples very unusual. There are some slightly curious aspects to the slides.

Figure 1 – The slide has a matt (the printed label surrounding the image) for TH McAllister, Manufacturing Optician, 49 Nassau Street, New York. This matt is identical to those used

---

1.   Illustrated in the Island Book Trust's publication 'Destination St Kilda', edited by the author. ISBN : 978-1-90744-03-9

by McAllister for their own slide production, except in small letters down the right hand edge it reads 'Made in Great Britain Expressly For TH McAllister, Manuf'g Optician'. This indicates that McAllister supplied GWW with pre-printed matts that were then used in slides destined to be part of the US companies stock. While it is difficult to read, hand written on the matt in white ink, below the image, it reads 'GWW' and above the image 'Group of St Kilda Women 6196'.

GWW often labelled his negatives within the image. This appears as white text against the dark background in the lower part of the image and is hidden behind the McAllister matt. If you look closely at the image of the back of the slide (**Figure 2**) it can be seen faintly just above the grey paper border. The label on this image reads 'Maids and Matrons, St Kilda 6196 G.W.W.'. There is also a hand written McAllister label on the back of the slide which reads 'Group of St Kilda Women'. So either GWW changed the name of the slide, for the American market, or whoever wrote the label made a mistake. In the UK series of lantern slides, this image is correctly labelled 'Group, with Queen' (**Figure 3**). Perhaps GWW thought it inappropriate to title one of the women as Queen, concerned that people in the USA might believe it referred to Queen Victoria.

Also, if you compare the US slide and UK slide (Figures 1 and 3) you will see that the US slide omits the woman on the extreme right of the image. At first sight, it seems like a cropping effect, making the image fit the USA oblong format rather than the UK format, but within the image seen on the back of the slide (Figure 2), see this woman appears on the slide, she is only obscured by the McAllister matt. The US slide was made at a slightly higher enlargement to the UK slide. If the same magnification has been used the woman would appear. I suspect the person making the US slide (they were always handmade) worked to fit the image to the width of the glass plate and didn't allow or adjust for the

*Figure 1. US format GWW lantern slide labelled
for TH McAllister – Front View*

*Figure 2. US format GWW lantern slide labelled
for TH McAllister – Back View*

Figure 3. UK format GWW lantern slide, hand coloured

matt covering part of the image. Whatever the reason, UK slide purchasers got more of the image than their US counterparts!

McAllister's catalogue from 1891 and 1898 lists a Scottish slide section, but all the Scotland slides with people in the images appear under the general title 'Life Studies, etc.'. There are two identifiable images from the 'Destination St Kilda' set, namely 'The St. Kilda Parliament.' and 'St. Kilda Women'.

The 1898 McAlister catalogue also advertises:

Detailed Catalogues of Foreign Views

Uncolored Photographs, on glass 3¼ inches wide, with protecting cover glass. –50c. each $45.00 per 100.

As it is impossible within the limits of this Catalogue to print a complete list of all the Foreign Views we can furnish, we will forward full catalogues of the Principal Foreign Makers, to those desiring same.

Price of each catalogue, 10c, including G. W. Wilson & Co., of Aberdeen Scotland: —Cathedrals and Abbeys of England and Scotland, and large assortment of Scotch Landscapes and Historic Buildings, among them many admirable views illustrating the History of Scotland, Poems of Burns, and Works of Sir Walter Scott.

In the same catalogue, McAllister explained in detail about sending their own photographer to Ireland in the summer of 1891 to take photographs. The photographer covered 3100 miles and took over 800 negatives of every part of the country. '*The slides are in standard 3 1/4" x 4" size, thus presenting a larger, handsomer picture than the old fashioned round mats, in which the imported views made in Ireland, were mounted*'. It is probable that the huge interest in Ireland was due to the large migration of the Irish to the US in the second half of the 19th century. There is no mention of a similar trip to Scotland, but the Scottish emigrants would have represented another obvious market.

A measure of the importance of the American market can be judged by a quote from their 1890 catalogue. In a letter received from 'The Chicago Lantern Slide Club' they state '*I profess to be a good judge of a perfect lantern slide and but precious few can compare with your own make ... I am frequently asked "Where can we get slides like those 'Scotch'?"*'

The original GWW lantern slide catalogue of 1890 (**Figure 4**) lists the whole series of 67 slides featured in 'Destination St Kilda', showing the St Kilda images as slides 57 to 66 (**Figure 5**).

The 1890 catalogue only lists these slides, but the 1912 catalogue also lists three additional St Kilda slides available to

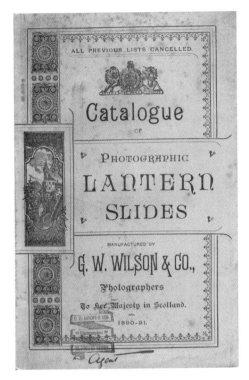

*Figure 4. Cover of GWW lantern slide
catalogue for 1890/91*

57 St. Kilda and Stack Lee.
58 Do.,   Town and Bay.
59 Do.,   Boreray.
60 Do.,   Parliament.
61 Do.,   Hunting Fulmar.
62 Do.,   Gannets' Nests.
63 Do.,   West Coast.
64 Do.,   Dividing Fulmar.
65 Do.,   Maidens and Matrons.
66 Do.,   Group, with Queen.

*Figure 5. Detail from 1890/91 catalogue showing
St Kilda slides in the 'Destination St Kilda' set*

185

1729	6190	St. Kilda, the Town and Bay, from the W.
1728	6202	Do., Burial Ground.
1729	6206	Do., Island of Boreray.

Figure 6. Detail from 1890/91 catalogue showing
additional St Kilda slides available

purchase separately (**Figure 6**). I have not seen the first two
images in UK lantern slide format, although the plate labelled
6190 is a more common view of the village in print format than
the photograph taken from the east which was included in the
'Destination St Kilda' set.

Image 6206 is actually the slide included in the 'Destination
St Kilda' set. I do not know why it is also listed here separately as
the other images in the set are not listed.

Figures 7 & 8 – shows that as well as producing slides for the
McAllister Company, GWW also made their own slides for the
US market and sold them through agents in the USA. The UK
size image shown of 'Town and Bay, St Kilda' is also part of the
'Destination St Kilda' slide set. The US sized slide more clearly
shows the white lettering above and below the image. This slide
is titled 'The Town and Bay, St Kilda from S, 6192'. This is exactly
the same text which appears in the negative.

Figure 9 – Another GWW slide for the US market, titled 'The
Town and Bay, St Kilda from NW, 6203'. GWW advertised this
slide in the UK format but I have not yet seen an example.

The George Washington Wilson Company went into
liquidation in 1902. Norman Macleod the photographer took
out copyright on a number of his images through 1901 and 1902.
Of the St Kilda photographs he copyrighted five images as far as
I am aware. They were 'Dividing the Catch', 'St Kilda Parliament',
'Gannets Nests', 'Maidens and Matrons' and 'The Burial Ground'.
Today these include the most famous images we know from the
GWW series. Perhaps even in 1902 they were recognised by
Macleod as the best or most important images.

Figure 7. GWW lantern slide produced in the US format

*Figure 8. GWW lantern slide produced in the UK format
and hand coloured*

Figure 9. GWW lantern slide produced in the US format

GWW gave a catalogue number to all his original plates and although there were duplications of plates, in general the numbers were only used once. The lowest catalogue number in the St Kilda series I know is '6187 The Glen' and the highest is '6206 The Island of Boreray'. This would mean there were probably at least 20 images originally. Today I know the title of only 13 of these images. Although I have not exhaustively researched the available prints in libraries and collections, I do know it is unlikely they existed as lantern slides as they never feature in the GWW catalogues.

However, as a final twist, GWW advertised:

These sets have been carefully made up from the best plates in the series of the various districts illustrated, while the readings –not too long and not too dry – will be found suitable for popular audiences. In the event of a lecturer wishing to illustrate more fully any particular district, G.W.Wilson & Co. would direct attention to their catalogue of over 12,000 views – any of which can be had, to order, as a Lantern Slide.

They maintained this offer until the business finally closed in 1908, by which time they had 65,000 plates. So, if someone was interested they could have ordered a lantern slide of any St Kilda images by Norman MacLeod and also, on request, have them hand coloured.

My search for further examples continues…

Recent Visitors to St Kilda: Attitudes, Perceptions and Responses

Jeff Stone

This modest contribution to the proceedings of the conference arose from an approach at a St Kilda Club reunion, suggesting that I talk on the subject of the motivations behind membership of the Club. The origins of the Club go back to the first National Trust for Scotland (NTS) work parties in 1958, but it was not formally constituted until 1976, whilst the St Kilda Mail commenced publication in 1977. The thirty-four subsequent issues of the Club's annual journal are, however, only a very indirect indicator of what motivates the membership which now numbers over 1,000 world-wide. The Mail keeps members informed about St Kilda and frequently includes historical records, but is rarely explicit on the thoughts or concerns of members about St Kilda. Their interest in St Kilda derives most commonly, but not exclusively, from work party experience and they self-evidently have a continuing interest in conservation on St Kilda, but it is difficult to say more from written records and without resorting to anecdotal evidence.

I therefore suggested to the conference organisers that I adopt a wider remit, namely the responses of 'recent visitors' rather than Club members, thus allowing me to search for sources beyond the Club records and publications. I was also proposing an approach which conforms more closely to the theme of the conference, by looking to see if the sorts of problems encountered in interpreting the historical literature are to be found in recent writing. With this intention in mind, I did not propose to consider anecdotal evidence, but only what I could find in written texts, formally published or not.

With hindsight, my revised proposal proved over-ambitious in terms of the extent of the literature search that I was able to undertake. My sources were the archives of the National Trust for Scotland in Edinburgh and in the Inverness office of the Trust, as well as St Kilda Club and private holdings, where newspaper and magazine articles on St Kilda are filed. The responses of visitors to St Kilda may be found in a very wide range of books, magazines and newspapers and it was not possible to search systematically through many such sources on the off chance. Hence, collections of cuttings were my main source. There are journal articles referenced in the St Kilda bibliography which I have not been able to consult. My findings are by way of a preliminary investigation and in so far as almost everyone must be aware of contemporary responses to St Kilda, perhaps this presentation may be a catalyst for others to contribute.

Further definitional problems remained at the outset. How recent is 'recent' and when is a visitor not a visitor (a word which implies a relatively brief and cursory stay)? Looking for a significant time period, an appropriate deadline is suggested by a theme of the conference, the evaluation of the many descriptions of St Kildan society written by outsiders. Post evacuation accounts are no longer commentaries on St Kildan society, but their consideration allows comparative questions to be posed, questions which may assist in the evaluation of the pre-evacuation literature. Are post evacuation accounts any more or less objective? Are they more or less emotive? Do recent accounts also support prior assumptions? Do the old myths die hard? For my purpose I therefore include any post August 1930 account as within my remit.

On the question of who is a visitor, I am conscious of hearing it said by personnel in employment on St Kilda that *'we are the St Kildans now'*. How long does a person have to stay on St Kilda to be declassified as a visitor? As I am looking at the post evacuation literature, for my purpose, every post 1930 account is potentially relevant, however short or long the authors have been on St Kilda. They are all part of what one eminent recent author describes as *'today's lively community of transients'*. That said, authors' circumstances are significant in shaping their responses to St Kilda, whether they came to the islands in the course of employment or by personal choice. Hence in looking at the various accounts, I group them by the origins of their visit, as a researcher, soldier, work party volunteer, yachtsman, etc.

Much of the post evacuation literature rules itself out for my purposes, in that it does not provide evidence of writers' personal views, other than by implication. The major monographs such as Emery, Harman, Williamson and Boyd, Fleming and Love self-evidently reveal a deep interest and commitment to St Kilda but statements of the authors' personal perceptions would be inappropriate. My archival sources are mainly more ephemeral, cuttings of newspaper and magazine articles, although they do include a small proportion of diaries and books, all sources where authors were concerned to state their personal views. I lost count of the total number of items consulted, many them using superlatives such as 'awesome' without any indication of the subject of their awe. I found comment in which the subject is evident in about one hundred texts, quite a few repetitive of others, and written by many different kinds of visitors. I offer a few sample comments from each category of visitor, but recognise that this is far short of a representative sample of the many thousands of visitors who have landed on St Kilda since 1930, most of whom do not record their thoughts.

I begin with the post evacuation 1930s. In that context I was reminded that the steamer service to St Kilda continued until the war, with the *Hebrides* and the *Dunara Castle* continuing to visit St Kilda several times in the summer. It is, perhaps, worth noting that despite the evacuation, demand remained, that St Kilda did not lose its tourist attraction in the absence of almost all the St Kildans. The earliest post evacuation report that I found was written by the Purser of the *Hebrides* and dated 11 September 1930, only a few days after evacuation. The vessel '*arrived at the now depopulated island of St Kilda at 2pm today. The weather was perfect and the landing and embarking of passengers by ship's boats were safely and satisfactorily effected. The absence of human life on the island was pathetic in the extreme…*'. This was perhaps an understandable response so soon after evacuation by a regular visitor who was accustomed to the bustle of a ship's visit. A less predictable response is to be found in a remarkable diary of typescript and photographs entitled 'Cruise to the Lone Island of St Kilda' by Elizabeth Ferguson in July 1931 and covering the entire cruise. The diary has recently been deposited in the archives of the National Trust for Scotland. The author states that '*I had looked forward tremendously to visiting St Kilda but whether or not it was the tossing we got coming over, or the very depressing day (it just hovers between heavy mist and real rain) but I could not get up much enthusiasm … we found everything very desolate and sad … the cemetery looked so forlorn and forgotten…*'. Perhaps an understandable reaction less than a year after evacuation, but a similar response is to be found seven years later, in 1938, when Robert Atkinson spent two weeks on St Kilda. His is the response of an ornithologist with a concise style, no romanticist, but he finds it a melancholy place: '*the queerness of no life sometimes pressing … all the trappings of a human colony but no humans*'. The absence of the St Kildans is very much in the minds of visitors in the 1930s, it seems.

Diarists are perhaps a category of respondent in their own right in that they are very likely to consider and record their feelings to supplement the daily record of what they are doing. They are compiled quite frequently by work party volunteers and I am indebted to a member of five recent work parties for allowing me access to her personal diaries which provides an interesting comparison with that of Elizabeth Ferguson. These later diaries are detailed accounts of day to day happenings, largely factual in nature. Any occasional emotions that are expressed are in respect of natural events such as the evening light on Dun, a brocken-spectre seen from the summit of Ruaival, a great skua taking a snipe or the discovery of a rock pipit's nest. The diarist does mention the St Kildans quite frequently, but in a matter of fact way, e.g. 'the St Kildans used it for…'. The emotion of the evacuation is not in evidence.

The post-1957 views of services personnel are on record, both in printed texts and on the St Kilda website, where they have been frequent contributors. They are often enthusiastic about their time on St Kilda. This is possibly a reaction to life on the MoD base, rather than to Hirta. The oft-quoted reaction is that troops either loved it or hated it. To Capt. Cooper it is 'one of the most beautiful places left'. To Lt.-Col. Stoddart it was not for the faint hearted: 'it was a rough, tough place and it still is'. More amusing is James McKay's account of 'the brutal and licentious soldiery taking up crochet, knitting, embroidery, painting by numbers and photography'. The latter was certainly the case. Crews of the landing craft which supplied St Kilda all year recall St Kilda predominantly in terms of their experiences of the weather and sea conditions as 'mean, moody and majestic'. As to be expected, there is no predominant response across the spectrum of military personnel. Some enjoyed the work because it was 'interesting and *unusual*, some enjoyed the island and some enjoyed life on the base. No doubt there are many not on record who would have responded adversely, had they been asked to do so.

The civilian employees on the base following the departure of the military might be expected to have a slightly different attitude to St Kilda, with a greater degree of choice than conscripts. Certainly some take a more assertive and positive attitude: '*we are a part of St Kilda ... people think of the history of St Kilda but there is a present day community*', and in a similar vein: '*we are the new St Kildans ... don't appreciate visitors coming over all judgemental about the radars*'.

Another category of transients who are sometimes inclined to differentiate themselves from mere visitors, are visiting scientists. By the nature of their published work, they tend not to report their personal responses to St Kilda, but one who did was D R Macgregor of Edinburgh University who compiled a large scale ground survey of Village Bay in April 1957 for the NTS. The man who taught me the rudiments of ground survey and was no romanticist recalls that St Kilda '*assails the senses, captivates the mind and leaves an impression that is deep and intimate*'. He found '*the island a wilder and more hostile place than I expected*', but goes on to say that '*it seems a strange contradiction that in spite of the hostility of the environment, I think of St Kilda as a homely place*', a contradiction which he explains by the sense of security afforded by the location of the village. The current Property Manager recalls her first impression of Glen Bay in her professional capacity as an archaeologist as '*a terrible place – loathe to go back*'. That was in bad weather, but returning in better weather: '*what a fantastic place*'! Peoples' responses will always be affected by the specific circumstances and that may also be true in a broader sense of the response of Timothy Bagenal, a marine biologist who organised the scientific expedition with Morton Boyd in 1952, who returned as a temporary Warden

195

during Operation Hardrock and again on a work party. Much later in 2003 he deplores what he calls the rape of St Kilda by the RAF and the Army and raises the question: '*has it also been raped by the NTS?*' He refers to the NTS as '*an organisation which wants to bring in hordes of people to have a holiday there while also doing Good Works*'. He shares the view of the Earl of Dumfries '*that St Kilda's ecosystems should not be disturbed*'. Another archaeologist who excavated on St Kilda, Mary Macleod, offers the perceptive comment that '*our perception of the isolation of St Kilda is what makes it particularly interesting, not the reality which is that it was part of the Hebrides where the archaeological record is more complete*'.

Cruise visitors are prolific sources of responses. Many use superlatives without saying what it is that induced them to say 'mind-blowing' or 'awesome'. Those who are more precise are usually referring to the cliff scenery and the stacks, but another common reaction is dismay at the sight of the base. In that particular context, it is apparent that for visitors whose stay on Hirta is longer than the average cruise visitor, a degree of acceptance sets in. There is a '*realisation that St Kilda is no longer a lonely outpost … the twenty-first century has been grafted on to an older St Kilda … there is a need to filter one's perceptions of the islands' remoteness and inaccessibility*'. Another thoughtful comment from a cruise visitor is that '*the fascination is the compound of interest, dramatic physiography, unique wildlife and a one-time independent community*'. A recent visitor offers the reminder that St Kilda is increasingly a tourist destination, commenting that they found it '*refreshingly void of the trappings of mainstream tourism – no handrails, signposts, walkways, cafés*'.

An element of romanticism is evident in the responses of more than one category of visitor. A cruise visitor who landed from the *Hebridean Princess* felt '*an overwhelming sense of melancholy for a lost way of life on an enchanted island*'. It is an attitude which is developed to a high order in the text accompanying Monica Weller's small book of photographs, in which the author is apparently in search of a spiritual or mystical experience, armed with a belief in a way of life which was in complete harmony with nature. Her short visit leads her to contemplate the meaning of life and, needless to say, her spiritual needs are gratified in a place where '*rare peace and naturalness of lifestyles is almost impossible to describe*'. Her response is in contrast to that of an official visitor, Patricia Ferguson MSP and Culture Minister, who described it as a privilege to be on St Kilda.

NTS work party volunteers might be expected to have their own characteristic responses to St Kilda. They are on Hirta for longer than many visitors and are likely to be similarly motivated. A common response is perhaps contained in the words of one work party member on departure: '*jealousy that another work party has arrived to invade "our" island*'. The possessive syndrome which is not unique to work party visitors can set in after a two week captivating stay. Another common view among work parties which contains a significant additional element is that '*it is not just scenery, wildlife and buildings but the people on the island which makes it a great experience*', a tribute to people employed on the island that work parties come in daily contact with. A predictable response is exemplified by another work party member, Lea MacNally, who speaks of '*the satisfaction of achievement after much endeavour*'. It's a theme which was developed obliquely in an amusing newspaper article by Pete and Rosy Almond who describe themselves as '*knackered for most of the fortnight*' before '*going for the mutiny option*', but doing so '*in the most fantastic place I have ever seen*'. Work parties do seem to be conducive to a particular form of response, namely free verse. Perhaps work party members have more time than some other visitors to contemplate their response to their surroundings and to set them in verse.

Visiting yachtsmen and kayakers might also be expected to produce their own characteristic responses to St Kilda. For yachtsmen it seems to be the challenge of the voyage to St Kilda rather than the islands themselves, which are an incidental bonus at best. Kayakers do seem to have their own response to the cliff scenery, deriving from their diminutive craft: *'kayaking around St Kilda gave me a unique perspective – nothing quite prepared me for the vertical scale of the cliffs'*. Other kayakers respond similarly.

Another category of writer which was referred to in cautionary terms by our key-note speaker is the professional journalist and author. They are not necessarily concerned to record their own impressions, of course, but they are concerned to produce copy which they believe will interest their readers. Jay Griffiths writing in the *Guardian* in 1998 is characteristic in looking for the odd and the idiosyncratic. She describes the NTS work parties as made up of *'chipper volunteers'* who are *'engaged in awfully obsessive preservation'*, *'living in restored cottages to restore more cottages'*. She mentions the bus stop which used to stand at the top of the hill in imaginative terms, *'where long queues of tourists have been known to wait for hours'* (really?). Amanda Hooton writing in the *Scotsman* in 1998 created fantasies around the people she met, including a woman with a magnetic field and another obsessed with sedges. She describes the St Kildans as *'refusing modern medicine and dying in catastrophic numbers of minor ailments'*. Eric Newby, who was on the island for approximately five hours in 1994 and published a two page article in the *Telegraph* records his first impression as *'a memorial to another world'* which he goes on to describe in a derived account from well known sources with his own occasional interpretation such as the St Kildans *'launching themselves into the abyss on home made straw* (sic) *ropes'*. He writes of *'the women and girls going to Boreray'* and concludes with the strange statement that *'almost everything about the St Kildans is a mystery'*. The factual detail of newspaper articles is perhaps unimportant in that the articles are more ephemeral than published books, unless they reinforce old myths or even create new ones, which is conceivable. Andrew Bailey writing in the *Sunday Times* in 1992 suggests that St Kildans had neither clocks nor calendars, had never seen a tree, only made contact with the mainland by means of a message in a bottle, before seventy (*sic*) villagers were evacuated in 1930. The whole impression created by the article is of a much more isolated and parochial community than they surely ever were.

My last category is the St Kildans themselves and their descendants returning to visit St Kilda. The descendants of the nineteenth century emigrants do write about their visits with genuine, constrained emotion which they experienced when standing among the houses on the street. The returning St Kildans mostly expressed similar sentiments and were surprised to find so much activity. They were happy to find people on St Kilda, despite any personal sadness which they felt and thought that the change was for the better.

An overview of all of the visitors' responses which I was able to consult, regardless of origins, provides an indication of what it is that excites recent visitors to St Kilda, what it is that impels them to put pen to paper. My sample is very small and far from fully representative, but it is possibly indicative. Visitors write about a range of topics, but the most frequent subject is St Kilda's cliff scenery. Reflections on pre-evacuation St Kildan society takes second place and after that it is the visual impact of the base, whilst the wildlife is in fourth place. Other topics which make an impression on visitors, in no particular order, include pleasure at contacts with people encountered on St Kilda, concerns about the MoD presence on St Kilda, concerns about increasing public access and rising visitor numbers, delight in sunsets and moonlight over Village Bay, the realisation that St Kilda's history does not end in 1930, the sheer satisfaction of getting there and the sadness in leaving. It seems that the cliff scenery is now what makes the greatest impression on visitors, but it is interesting that so many features of St Kilda excite visitors.

In conclusion, do the responses of post evacuation visitors differ in any discernable way to the pre-evacuation reports? Many of the post evacuation reports are quite emotive, with frequent use of superlatives, but perhaps that is to be expected of the small proportion of visitors who seek to express their feelings. Superficially it seems to me that, if anything, recent visitors are more impressed with what they see than pre-1930 visitors, although I doubt if such a simple comparison is entirely valid, if only because the cultural context changed with the passage of time. Occasionally it does seem that recent visitors have their own preconceptions and they find what they seek, whether or not it matches what others observe. Do the old myths die hard and are new myths created? Not conspicuously so, but what is apparent is that anything in print, particularly in the more popular sources, is likely to be plagiarised and sometimes exaggerated or otherwise distorted for dramatic effect. Steel is more likely to be quoted than Fleming. That said, most writers seem motivated to respond to what they observe in a genuine manner, albeit on a range of topics, whether it is the magnitude of the human footprint, the majesty of the scenery or the convivial people they meet. Much clearly depends on the physical circumstances of their visit and its duration, but the vast majority can probably be accepted at face value.

I am tempted to conclude by projecting back in time and suggesting that not much has changed when one looks across the pre and post evacuation literature of St Kilda. Visitors inevitably write from their own individual circumstances. Recent visitors who write about St Kilda are numerous enough to be confident that they do so from a range of different perspectives, circumstances and motivations which certainly influence their responses. Perhaps this may also be said of the literature of the pre-evacuation period. If there is any validity in this suggestion, then there is nothing unusually insidious about the corpus of pre-evacuation literature of St Kilda. The pre-1930 literature of St Kilda requires no more care or discretion in its interpretation than any other documentary source.

A St Kilda Diary

David Boddington

D avid Boddington was meant to be launching his book on the morning of the third day of the conference. However, it had been available on the previous two days and many of the audience in the room had already read parts of it. John Randall, who was in the chair for the talk, therefore promised to move things along to free up time afterwards for relaxation and an opportunity for some people to continue their reading of the book.

In relation to much of what had been heard from other speakers the topic was relatively recent, but it was pure fact from fifty years ago. His diary was started on August 25th 1958 when he first set foot on the landing craft that was to take him over from Stranraer, past the Mull of Kintyre and the south end of Islay to Village Bay on St Kilda. He was due to take over the medical equipment and quarters from the Royal Army Medical Corps quartermaster who was from Glasgow. The summers of both 1957 and 1958 had been ones of constant activity on St Kilda for members of the Royal Air Force unit who were using their wartime experience in setting up nissen huts, building roads, blasting in the quarry, and providing stout buildings for generators.

Because of weather changes and a S.O.S. message that had to be obeyed, the sailing and disembarkation plans went askew with some drama. To an extent this was a foreboding of a wet landing three days later; and many more exciting landings with smaller boats on rarely used cliff sites, and even at the pier next to the buildings used by the medical unit. Once the last September landing craft tank had pushed itself up onto the sandy beach and got off on the high tide, the wintering party of twenty-five soldiers was entirely reliant on what it had stored in reserve, what the supply boat *Mull* would bring (its human and nautical limitations were numerous) and whatever we could get from her to the pier in our small boat. Our mail used to arrive by Fleetwood trawler about two or three times a month, and had to be fetched from the ship as it stood off-shore.

Most soldiers were on for six week spells, and seniors from the guided weapons unit in Benbecula and South Uist would make overnight visits. But these movements were controlled by the weather and tides. Every soldier was expected to turn his hands and mind to help others, and rank and corps did not count. The leader at any time or event emerged with recognised qualities. The commanding officer was a gunner, and his main practical support was from the Royal Electrical and Mechanical Engineers (REME), with their electronic skills.

The only other commissioned officer was a doctor who had been qualified for two years. He had done two hospital jobs with experience in casualty work and a year at a military hospital in Glasgow. With Scottish Command he had experience of winter conditions in the Cairngorms, and had also done a short course in dentistry. He had been agitating for this posting since starting National Service and was destined to stay a year with a two week break. He had a medical team of two, both with nursing experience – the sergeant, a man of great human skill with the young soldiers, some fresh from home in urban areas; and a private who had a higher national diploma in engineering.

The medical officer was also the catering officer with two catering corps cooks who were exempt from boat work as at all times of day or night they were at hand with sustenance. The medical officer was authorised to issue rum if needed!! He was also trusted with the sharp scissors when hair trimming was ordered or asked for!! His sergeant ran the bar!! The private sometimes helped with the coded thrice daily weather reports which the medical officer then sent to Benbecula airport. These were used, together with weather maps made up from the 7:55 morning shipping forecast, to brief the firing range and any visiting ships. The private was also the first to sort the mail when it arrived in the medical room, having a good eye for official mail for either of the two officers. This helped in getting hasty replies back on to the boat.

Spanish trawlers would frequently shelter in the bay. Their crews would often give fish and wine in exchange for stewing beef. Once, they landed a team to play darts and snooker, failing to recognise Glaswegian dialect as English, but still winning.

There was a trained plumber, carpenter, seaman, and two signallers who could use Morse code, voice (very crackly) semaphore and pistol – fired lights. Three generator attendants did eight hour shifts and there were three or four REME radar experts and an electrician.

The overlaps were left to the lads – most would try to learn the skills of others. Soon, the radar images of birds thought during the war to be 'angels', were explained by the medical officer. As a perk, he was able to do some original research on radar images of sea birds feeding. He also represented the National Trust for Scotland – the owner of the island group – and the Nature Conservancy Council which was responsible for the protection of the important fauna and flora.

The medical officer was the only one to be there with his own interests in mind, but there were a few who were prepared to go out with him, not only to help but learn. Contacts like this, and the feelings picked up by the listening ears of the junior medics, were of use in ascertaining the mental pulse of the unit. We all mingled in the bar most evenings, where words that were too relaxed for comfort were forgotten by the next day. There was a film about every ten days, with appreciative comments when girlfriend substitutes appeared on them.

Army postings had the reputation for being devoid of constructive and sympathetic thought, but several years later many seemed to have benefited in having got good jobs. There were no terrible accidents in the first year, but one rocket created a near miss; and there were periods of immersion in the sea during efforts to get boats out or in. But, as this was a matter of mail or no mail, most were keen to achieve success, and there was always a rope to hold on to.

One has to look for humour in most situations, and if some is found it is that which is retained in the memory, rarely the pain. The medical officer described the experience as an untypical transect through his medical career. To others it has marked their whole life – a combat with natural forces but without any bullets. The diaries from which the book and these comments have been taken give a detailed account of the first year of the re-occupation of St Kilda. This enabled the effective operation of the guided weapons range on Benbecula and South Uist about fifty miles away.

It is fifty years since the diarist left St Kilda which lies, appropriately, fifty miles from the nearest land: coincidental historical and geographical figures.

The Literature of the Great Blasket (An Blascaod Mor): An Extraordinary Output

Mícheál de Mórdha

The Blasket Islands are a group of islands off Slea Head (Ceann Sleibhe) on the tip of the Dingle peninsula in south-west Ireland. There are six islands in the group, the main one of which is Great Blasket Island. It is located about three miles across Blasket Sound from the mainland though the nearest point, at Dunmore Head, is just one mile away. The islands have been called *Next Parish America*. They are situated in one of the most beautiful panoramas in the world. Though they are close to the mainland they have a sense of the mysterious and exude a feeling of remoteness. This is exacerbated by the frequent times when they are shrouded in mist and cannot be seen from the mainland.

Great Blasket Island has probably been inhabited from Neolithic times. However, there were probably not many people living on the island until the end of the nineteenth century and the beginning of the twentieth century. There is much evidence of human occupation, ranging from the ring fort of An Dun to the discovery of an anchor from a Viking boat. A more dubious source – a Spanish surveyor's account of 1579 refers to inhabitants in the area all speaking Spanish! Verifiable written accounts of the island's history are available from the early eighteenth century onwards.

The island was acquired by the Cambro-Norman household of the Desmond Geraldines after coming to Ireland in 1169. It was administered for a long period by the Feiritear (Ferriter) household who came with the Normans and settled around Ballyferriter. The annual rental was reputed to be a number of hawks and, in ancient accounts the islands are referred to as 'Ferriter's Islands'. The House of Desmond rebelled against the forces of the English crown and that of Elizabeth the First in particular in the latter part of the sixteenth century. However, the rebellion was mercilessly put down and the vast lands of the earldom. Including the remote Blasket Islands, were subsequently acquired by the Boyles, the 'New English' Earls (later Lords) of Cork. The Ferriters fell out of favour with the English ascendancy and most of their lands, including the Great Blasket, were forfeited.

Pierce Ferriter was hanged by the English in 1653. The Lords of Cork took over possession of the island. And their agents, like Sam Hussey, collected rents – which were often exorbitant. Unsurprisingly, Blasket people often resisted paying their rent and on one occasion, in 1891, their boats were seized because of rent default after being invaded by the British warship *Britomart*. Their boats were subsequently ransomed. The island was sold by Lord Cork to the Irish Congested Districts Board (CDB) in 1907 for £600. On the establishment of the Irish State, the functions of the CDB were transferred to the Irish Land Commission. The freehold of 66 fields was eventually given to island families. 90% of the island was commonage with each family having a one twenty-fifth share in it.

The island was populated by people moving over from the mainland. The population of Ireland increased rapidly in the first half of the nineteenth century. This was a time of unscrupulous landlords and the subdivision of farms. Land on the mainland was becoming scarce whilst the islands were relatively immune from persecution by land agents. At a time of mainland want Great Blasket was a great fishing base. Rabbits and seabirds also abounded and provided additional food sources – gannets, puffins and fulmars. However, the island suffered from a lack of services – no medical personnel, no shop or church, no electricity and running water. It was virtually isolated from the mainland and the only means of regular contact was in the islanders' canoes (naomhoga). Island men went out to sea and the women took care of the home and children. It was a monoglot Irish-speaking community and the islanders always went 'in' to the island and 'out' to the mainland. They survived by fishing and some farming – crafting – especially of sheep. A bartering system was operated in which no money was necessary – the community being more important than the individual. They cared for one another in bad times and were a God-fearing community although there was no clerical presence on the island. However, they did have their own 'Dail' – an 'assembly' or 'parliament'.

The people had no radio or television and no telephones. There were occasional newspapers. The islanders spent much of their time fishing and farming. They were noted for their music and song. Dancing and house visiting (bothantaiocht) were frequent as was storytelling – an oral tradition developed into an art form. Visits were made to the mainland for provisions and also to attend christenings, weddings, funerals, cattle fairs, regattas and so forth. There are accounts of the island community from nineteenth century visitors. Not all are complimentary. Mrs D. P. Thompson, the wife of a reviled local land agent, wrote in her book, published in 1846, that '*there are about 150 inhabitants on the great Blasquett; these people are in a state of extreme ignorance, not a single individual in the island could read a word of English ...*

not any religious service was hitherto performed in the island.[1] In 1911 there were 160 people (83 males and 72 females) on the island, falling to 110 (64 males and 46 females) by 1936 and ten years later to only 45 (32 males and 13 females). At the 1911 census 50% of the population was aged 18 and under and only 8% aged 65 and over.

There have been two schools on the island. One was a 'soup school' set up by proselytising Protestants (the islanders were Catholics). It opened the islanders' minds to the world of learning and literature. Irish and English were taught in the school as well as Catechism. An Irish language primer 'An Cat Breac' (Speckled Cat) was used in the school. The Protestant educational and proselytising drive lasted for a decade or so, from 1839 to 1850. It was the islanders' first experience of formal education. The Blasket expert, Muiris Mac Conghail, reckons '*the bible reading activity and the basic teaching of reading and writing … must account for some of the literacy skills which the community acquired*'. After the Protestant school closed the islanders were without any schooling for about fourteen years. A National (Catholic) school was opened in 1864 with assistance from catholic clergy. This school opened their minds to life outside the island. There was an emphasis on teaching through English. Irish was not formally taught. In its early years the school had no teacher on occasions because of the island's remoteness and other factors. At one stage there were some sixty children and two teachers attending. The school closed in 1941 when there were only six pupils attending and one teacher. It was one of '*the straws that broke the camel's back*'.

Storytelling was one of the principal ways in which the islanders amused themselves. Stories were transmitted from

---

1.   D. P. Thompson, *A Brief Account of the Rise and Progress of the Change in religious Opinion Now Taking Place in Dingle and the West of the County of Kerry, Ireland* (London, 1846).

generation to generation for many generations. Stories were embellished and developed over time and storytellers were held in high regard. One woman islander related over 300 stories to a folklore collector. There were several types of oral tradition. 'Fiannaiocht' – old stories of the great deeds of Fionn Mac Cumhail and Na Fianna – were usually the preserve of men. Some were very long and embellished. There were also stories pertaining to the community, customs, 'piseoga' etc; and scary stuff of the other world, 'pucai' etc. And there were also prayers and incantations.

At the beginning of the twentieth century scholars became interested in the island. There was an upsurge of interest in Irish (which was in rapid decline) and everything 'Irish'. Because of their isolation the islanders spoke a very pure form of Irish. They had not been interrupted by outside influences for a long time. Some of the early scholars included: the American Jeremiah Curtin, a folklore collector; the Irish playwright John Millington Synge; Karl Marstrander (Norwegian); Robin Flower and George Thomson (both English); and the Irishmen Brian O Ceallaigh and Padraig O Siochfhradha 'An Seabhac'. The most important scholars either knew or learned Gaeilge (Irish). The islanders readily recited their stories to them and, in turn, the scholars realised that the islanders 'spoke' great literature. The islanders were also urged to write their stories and 'put pen to paper'.

There was a trinity of Great Blasket main authors, namely: Tomas O Criomhthain (Thomas O' Crohan), Muiris O Suilleabhain (Maurice O' Sullivan) and Peig Sayers (Peg Sayers) who was born on the mainland. O Criomhthain was the pioneer and other authors followed. Peig Sayers could not write in Gaeilge and dictated her stories. The first edition of books were written in Gaeilge and later translated. O Criomhthain (1855–1937) was prompted by Marstander, Flower, O Ceallaigh and others. O Silleabhain (1904–1950) was 'adopted' by Thomson.

Peig Sayers's (1873–1958) stories were noted by many people. She had over 300 of them and eventually these were written down by her son, Micheal, known as 'An File' (The Poet) who also became an author.

O Criomhthain's classic *An tOileanach* (*The Islandman*) was first published in the original Gaeilge in 1929. His first book *Allagar na hlnise* (*Island Crosstalk*) was published in 1928. The literary merits of *An tOileanach* were instantly recognised. Translations followed. Urged by O Criomhthain's success Muiris O Suilleabhain published *Fiche Bliain ag Fas* (*Twenty Years A-Growing*) in 1933 with financial assistance from Thomson. Peig Sayers's autobiography *Peig* was published in 1936 followed by *Machnamh Seanmhna* (*An Old Woman's Reflections*). Other books followed, including books by O Criomhthain's and Peig Sayers's sons. In 1933 the *New York Times* review of Maurice O'Sullivan's *Youth and the Irish Islanders* brought international recognition.

From about 1930 to the present day, an extraordinary amount of books have been produced by either Blasket authors or by visitors to the island. There are also translations and other editions of these books. Several hundred articles about the island have also been published. All of this material is incorporated into what is now termed 'The Blasket Library'. Up to 2008 there had been thirty-two reprints of the Oxford University Press (OUP) edition of *The Islandman* – the English translation of An tOileanach. OUP published the first impression of their edition in 1951. There were other editions by other publishers before that and Blasket books are still appearing.

Just as the Blasket community became known worldwide through its literature, the community was in fatal decline. As visitors came in droves to the island, the islanders heard of a better life across the sea. The young people of the island left, leaving behind an aged community. Most of the Blasket emigrants settled in Springfield in Massachusetts in the USA. After the First World War, mackerel fishing declined around the island. The islanders had become accustomed to the idea of money being necessary for adding to their comforts. By the 1940s there were just about enough able-bodied men to provide for the aged community. The school closed in 1941 with only six pupils. A young man died of meningitis on the island in the early days of 1947. Nothing could be done for him because of the severe weather. The community realised it could not persevere any longer. It asked the Irish government for assistance and an inter-departmental committee was established. Great Blasket was abandoned in 1953. The Blasket Foundation was established in 1986 and the Blasket Centre built on the mainland within sight of the island village in 1992–93. Most of the land on Great Blasket was bought by the Irish government from private owners in January 2009. A management plan for the island has now been accepted by the government. Conservation of the island village is a priority. A guide service was introduced on Blasket in the summer of 2010 with great success.

Tomas O Criomhthain left his literary legacy because he wanted to '*set down the character of the people*' about him '*so that some record of us might live after us, for the like of us will never be again*'. It is doubtful if he ever realised that the island would, one day, be abandoned although he realised the community could not be sustained as it was in his own lifetime.

Faroese Writing

Bergljót av Skarði

My name is Bergljót av Skarði and I am a teacher at Føroya studentaskúli og HF skeið – a school for 16–19 year olds. My subjects are English and Faroese, which I have studied in Denmark and Faroes respectively being among the first ever to graduate from the Faroese University Fróðskaparsetur Føroya – Academia Faroensis (www.setur.fo). Our university was founded in 1965, but not till the seventies were they ready to start producing candidates.

Karl Dunganon, Duke of Sankt Kilda

The invitation to this conference was particularly interesting to me because it mentioned a trip to St Kilda. I have known about St Kilda since I was a child because in my family, and among my parents' friends, there are several *Knights of St Kilda* and many times would I hear jokes or stories involving 'the Duke of St. Kilda'. The title 'Knight of St Kilda' was presented to these people by a mystic called Carolus Dunganon (1897–1972) – or, as his Icelandic parents called him Karl Einarson. He grew up in Tórshavn so some of his knights were Faroese. He heard that titles were for sale in England and that St Kilda was uninhabited so he called himself Duke of St Kilda. He was also a poet, writing in 17 languages including Faroese, and on

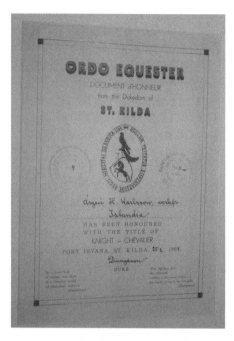

Document stating that the owner is Knight of St. Kilda

the cover of his book of poems it says 'Universal edition of St Kilda 1962'.[1]

Another memory of mine is of Shetland, its development resembling ours to such a great extent that in the Faroes we were warned by the Shetland horror example when we were corrected in our speech or, when in language lessons at school, we were told about the Shetland variety of Nordic – Norn, an extinct language.

Our subject today is Faroese literature, focusing on its role in preserving Faroese as an independent language. The lecture is arranged chronologically.

---

1. Dunganon: Corda Atlantica 1962.

Oral literature – before written literature[2]

Faroese is a Nordic language – a direct descendant from old Norse, its nearest kin being Icelandic and Western Norwegian. As far as declinations and word structure are concerned, Faroese places itself somewhere between the two as it has grown further away from the original than Icelandic but not as far as Norwegian.

Any discussion of Faroese language and literature must start with spoken language and oral tradition. All traditional oral genres are to be found in the Faroes: we have folk tales, fairy tales, legends, proverbs and such-like. But first and foremost we have ballads. The Faroe ballad treasure is particularly rich and varied. In fact the Faroes are unique in that respect – having preserved not only the ballads, but also the dance to go with them – although today's dancing is far from its heyday. The ring dance, which was widely used in Europe during medieval times, is nothing without the ballads, and the ballads not much without the dance, but together, as a perfectly integrated unity, they form a piece of culture which has proved itself strong enough to withstand centuries of change. The dance is performed without any other music than singing – singing long, dramatic, epic poems.

It is generally agreed that the ballads have served as the lifeline of the language during the massive influence on Faroese – preserving it in the rhyme, rhythm and drama of the thousands of stanzas learned by heart in every village on every island. The language of the ballads often found and still finds its way into spoken language. People would use quotations and sayings from a ballad in particularly important or solemn situations. We have lots of evidence that the ballad dancing was revered and that children were taught proper behaviour in the ring and to respect the singer.

---

2. Árni Dahl: Føroysk bókmentasøga I-III (Fannir 1980).

Our oldest ballads are from the 14th century. We don't know the author or authors, but their subject-matter originates in foreign countries far away from the Faroes. In many of the ballads characters and events correspond to those in the Old Icelandic sagas such as Vølsungasaga and Karlamagnusar saga, which were quite the literary trend during the 13th and 14th centuries. The old ballads are often very long – several hundred stanzas, and often you have large cycles containing several long ballads dealing with the same events from different points of view, with different main characters. Typically one ballad deals with a love triangle, and one of the suitors is killed, and the next ballad in the group deals with the revenge on the killer.

Our most famous ballad group or cycle is the Sjúrðarkvæðini – the Sigfried ballads – a distant kin to the Germanic Niebelungenlied. Around 1800 there was a revival in ballad making. The new ballads take their subject matter nearer to home, we have many ballads which explore the Føroyingasøga, which is an Icelandic saga dealing with the first settlers in the Faroes around the year 1000. It has two main characters, two main families competing for power. The ballad authors at this time of course would write down their songs, but books were few and far between so these ballads were also spread round the country in oral tradition, many people would write them down thus making their own personal collection of ballads.

Writing with no standard orthography

There is little written documentation of Faroese from the middle ages. Our most important document is the so-called Seyðabrævið (Sheep letter), a legal text concerning sheep farming, payment for lodgings and punishment for libel. The Seyðabrævið is from 1298. This document bears signs that Faroese at this time has developed its own variation of Old Norse as do placenames and personal names in land registers and church protocols, which together with the Seyðabrævið, are the only traces of early Faroese in written sources. The first writers of modern Faroese had no standard orthography so each of them wrote his own version. Sometimes we can trace dialect marks, for instance in J.C. Svabo who was from Vágoy.

The Faroese scholar **Jens Christian Svabo** (1746–1824) wrote a report (1781–82) from the Faroes. He reports on economics, culture, religion, superstition, and of particular interest are his comments on the Faroese language. His objective is purely scientific- antiquarian. He says that the language is in such a poor state, so many words have been forgotten and replaced by Danish words, and people are so careless about their speech that he is certain that Faroese will disappear. Therefore he will write down examples and collect vocabulary in order to let scientists know what Faroese was like; and to that end he composed a Faroese-Danish-Latin dictionary (in his own orthography). Luckily Svabo's bleak predictions have not come true yet, but his writings were an inspiration to others to start writing down ballads. During the 1800s a number of handwritten ballad collections were issued in different dialects – because in spite of their moderate size the Faroes have several distinct dialects.

The most important single event for the Faroese language must be the creation of a standard orthography. The year 1846 must be the most important date in the curriculum, and I tell my students that if they remember nothing else, they must remember 1846. The 'father of the orthography' is **Vencil Ulricus Hammershaimb** (1819–1909) a clergyman from Sandavágur in Vágoy. As a young student, he watched the injustice and indignity which the Faroese language suffered, for instance when, in 1844, Danish authorities decided to establish Danish schools in the Faroes although they were not wanted. Danish would be the language of instruction, the children would be taught

Danish history, Danish geography and so on, ensuring intensive Danification of children. Carl Julian Graba, a German lawyer from Kiel, has this comment on the education in the Faroes in 1828, i.e. before the Danish schools were implemented:

Each father teaches his own children the way he was taught by his parents, first and foremost reading, writing and religion, and with such good results that I – as I have stated earlier – would rather spend half a day with the Faroese than one hour with one of our peasants.[3]

Hammershaimb wrote a letter to a Danish newspaper in which he compared the situation of the Faroese language in the Faroes to that of the Danish language in Slesvig, demanding that the Danish grant the same rights to Faroese in the Faroes as they claim are due to Danish in Slesvig. The political significance of language policy and school policy evident in that letter is classical. Even today the political situation in the Faroes is such that discussions about language, orthography, loan-words etc. invariably turn political.

During visits to the Faroes while he was still a student in Copenhagen in the 1840s, Hammershaimb gathered and wrote down ballads, legends and other oral 'texts'. This way our first written literature was oral literature. Hammershaimb believed that the Faroese orthography should be founded on etymological principles, enabling you to see the connection to Old Norse and to our nearest neighbours – preserving the roots. We still use Hammershaimb's orthography. Hammershaimb also wrote a book of grammar thus giving the Faroese an important tool in the ongoing argument about the rights and justification for the existence of the Faroese language.

At this stage we have to introduce Jakob Jakobsen (1864–1918) whom I'm sure many of you know from his work in Shetland.

---

3.   Carl Julian Graba: Dagbók í árinum 1828 (Tórshavn 1987).

Dr Jakobsen wrote his doctoral thesis – he was the first person from the Faroes to become a doctor – on Norn, the Old Norse language in Shetland; thus giving Norn a headstone to its grave and scholars the opportunity to study what was once in Shetland. Shetland or Hetland as we say in Faroese is viewed with sadness in the Faroes. Look what happened to Shetland you'd hear teachers and linguists warn. Dr Jakobsen was an advocate of the trendy science phonetics, and in his opinion our orthography should be much closer to the pronunciation of the words. Although they differed much in their theoretical approach Dr. Jakobsen helped Hammershaimb with much of his work.

This dispute between etymology and phonetics had quite a serious impact on the cultural scene in the Faroes because it created a bitter strife in the Føringafelag and resulted in 1901 in the death of their magazine the Føringatíðindi which had tried to accommodate both parties.

Not reformation rather deformation

I can see in the conference programme that one of the questions on the agenda is the real role of the church. This is a very interesting point because in many cases the church in the Faroes – and I guess in many colonies or dependent countries – has exercised a very negative influence, stifling Faroese culture. The Faroese were for centuries traditionally Christian. They believed that God created everything and was in control, but they did not talk much about it or flaunt their faith or their personal salvation. A quotation from the French traveller Charcot from 1901 illustrates this point:

> *The Faroese believe in God but their protestant faith is much more liberal than that of the English. Saturday night they read the bible, Sunday they go to church, but the rest of the day they have fun just like Catholics. Sunday evening*

219

they dance, sometimes 'English' dances waltz, polka etc.,
sometimes their own dance; they dance in a ring with certain
dance steps while they sing songs about the famous Magnus
Heinason, dancing is the favourite pastime in the Faroes.[4]

Towards the end of the 19th century new more aggressively missionary religious communities reached the Faroes. Some of these condemned the Faroese dancing as sinful, which obviously was a major blow, given – as we have seen – its importance to the language and general identity building.

One of Martin Luther's main objectives was to introduce the vernacular into the church. Around Europe the Reformation resulted in bible translations and hymns translated into or written in each country's own language. In the Faroes, however, reaching us via Denmark reformation turned into deformation as the country was flooded with Danish clergymen and the Danish bible became the only bible allowed in church. However, we had clergymen, teachers and scholars who opposed this by translating the bible, translating hymns and conducting church services in places other than the church. And over a long period of time the bible was translated and hymns were created. But it was a long struggle both in school matters and in church matters.

Literature[5]

Faroese literature is not many generations old – a fact that makes my job as a teacher very personal. I have seen and talked with many of our major writers – even the classics. My grandfather was one of the founders of the Faroese folk high school which was the first, and for a long time, the only school teaching pupils

---

4.   Jean Charcot: Ferðir til Føroya 1934 (Sprotin 1994).
5.   Turið Sigurðardóttir: 'Fãrõisk litteratur' in Fãrõarna mer ãn fåglar (Norden 19).

their mother tongue. He also published the first children's magazine. My mother was active in protesting against the legal paragraph which barred Faroese from school as an instruction language. When my father-in-law (born 1906) was buried in the late eighties we sang Danish hymns in his honour because they were what he was used to. When he was young, there were no Faroese psalms, and there was no Faroese bible. The whole literary and linguistic curriculum seems very close which may add to the teacher's enthusiasm, but also may impair his or her objectivity.

Modern Faroese literature came into being in the 1870s when, for the first time, we had poetry written in Faroese. This was possible because one could use the linguistic and poetic traditions of the oral literature as a foundation, and there was an orthography in place. Scandinavian patriotic songs, which were blooming two decades earlier, served as a model. The patriotic movement arose among young Faroese students in Copenhagen in the 1870s, consequently *loss* and *longing for home* emerged as major themes. The poetry is closely linked to patriotism consisting mostly of praise for the country, history, people and language. The songs established what was specially Faroese, thus becoming one link in the creation of a conscious Faroese identity. From the turn of the century patriotism turned political in a more direct way, and the poetry developed into protest songs in favour of linguistic, cultural and political independence for the Faroes. The poets themselves were active in the cultural and political struggle for independence which is the foundation of today's modern society.

The Faroese patriotic movement in Denmark was soon adopted in the Faroes, and the end of the 19th and the beginning of the 20th century saw a lively growth in Faroese literature. The Føroyingafelag, a society for the advancement of Faroese language and the Faroese people, was started in 1889, and its meetings (fólkafundir) and the magazine Føringatíðindi – written in Faroese – was essential in the wave of literary creativity at the turn of the century. Fólkafundir (folk meetings) were held in the summer. Located in beautiful spots, in the mountains and valleys, they drew masses of people from all the villages nearby. People would come by boat or walking long distances. There would be a church service in Faroese, speeches and romantic songs – often made for that occasion.

One of the expressed goals of the Faroese Society was to establish a folk high school, and this was the first goal to be reached – in 1898. Símun av Skarði and Rasmus Rasmussen founded the Føroya fólkaháskúli, modelled on the Danish folkehøjskole, a school for the people, established in the wake of constitutional change in Denmark which required a more informed population. Also in Denmark it was part of a national democratising movement. As there were no books in Faroese available, Símun av Skarði and Rasmus Rasmussen provided the texts themselves. Most of the teaching was lectures, but they also wrote books, one of them specialising in the humanities and the other in natural sciences. As we have heard already, the folk high school had Faroese language, history and culture on its programme, and many writers later expressed their debt to this school with respect to their coming out as writers. The encouragement and training of the teachers had boosted their self confidence and strengthened their resolve to pursue a literary calling. For example, Martin Joensen (1902–1966) and Heðin Brú (1900–1987) – great story writers in the 1930s and 40s – have expressed as much.

There were firsts of everything – we have already mentioned first songs 1876; first drama for the stage 1889; first novel 1909; first short stories 1912 and first collection of poetry 1914.

The most important name in this period is Jóannes Patursson (1866–1946), a farmer at the historically important Kirkjubøur.

His powerful party songs are still in use. He had extensive knowledge about oral poetry and he is creative on ancient ground. The prehistoric North, our Norwegian ancestors and heroes from the old ballads and sagas are portrayed as models for the present. His poetry was at the service of the patriotic cause and a new sense of self-esteem was being sung into the people.

After the period of romantic songs, many of which are still included in the 'Songbók Føroya folks' (Songbook of the Faroese People) which is a household book in the Faroes, we see the emergence of a more introvert kind of poetry, poems which do not want to tell a story or carry a mission. Janus Djurhuus (1881–1948) and his brother Hans Andreas Djurhuus (1883–1951) are two of our most important writers. Janus Djurhuus, our earliest great and learned poet, published his first collection in 1914, the first collection of poetry in Faroese. He was educated in Denmark in law and classical languages, and his wide horizon is evident in his work as well as in his translations of the Iliad from Greek and others such as Goethe and Schiller. While Janus Djurhuus is a difficult poet, his younger brother Hans Andreas became the people's poet. He was a teacher, and his poetry for children was, and is, the first taste of poetic language for all children in the Faroes. He wrote in all genres but his nature lyrics and the children's poetry are classics – a continual inspiration to Faroese music composers.

A century and a half old, Faroese print literature arose as a vehicle for an ongoing differentiation from the Danish state. Born in reaction to the denial that such a thing as Faroese writing could exist or had any chance of superseding Danish as the official medium of the Faroe Islands, Faroese literature long developed as a continuous nationalist revival. Consequently, Faroese language writing, as such, cannot be separated from the original project of transforming an unlettered folk dialect into a national language and of ratifying this transformation in a literary canon. Much Faroese writing has been offered explicitly as a contribution to the heroic launching of a national literature, but any Faroese work of literature fills a slot. The Djurhuus brothers' contribution illustrates the extreme ends of the spectrum of literary nation-building: on one hand, the ambitious creation of high-literary works comparable to those of the national literatures against which Faroese literature measures its progress and, on the other hand, the devoted effort to fulfil the needs of a general readership.[6]

Most literary trends are to be found in the Faroese book production. Usually a trend will reach us some time after it has developed in the rest of Europe, but today with modern communications and media, the time lapse is continually growing shorter. The principles of the French Revolution took a hundred years to travel to the Faroes; naturalism in literature started in Denmark in the 1870s and in Faroese naturalism was evident in the first novel *Bábelstornið* (The Tower of Babel) from 1909. Modernism in form and content was first seen in 1963, having started in Scandinavia maybe 20 years earlier.

In Faroese literary history prose and poetry seem to take turns at dominating the scene. Prose had a blossoming between 1930 and 1950, by writers born around the turn of the century – Heðin Brú (1900–1987), Martin Joensen (1902–1966) and Willian Heinesen (1900–1991). **Heðin Brú** from Skálavík describes the transition from the old farmers' society to modern times when the fishing industry takes over. His novels – particularly Feðgar á ferð (in English, The Old Man and his Sons) and short stories give a warm and humourous description of the people of the old days in the Faroes, contrasting their peaceful village life to new technology and money society. **Martin Joensen** writes social realistic stories about people working on fishing vessels and

---

6. Faroese National Library – http://www.flb.fo

working on land in fish drying. He offers a broad view of the struggle between old and new and the class differences arising during the period when a new class of fishermen and another of shipowners emerge. **William Heinesen** is the most famous of all Faroese authors, and his work has been translated into many languages. He grew up in a merchant's home in Tórshavn in a partly Danish environment, and all his work was written in Danish. Ironically his international position differs a lot from his position at home. While all critics agree that he is an eminent writer of both poetry and prose, and his books give a humorous, highly artistic picture of the Faroes and the Faroese, he has been received somewhat coldly by his countrymen. The fact that he wrote his books in Danish may have alienated him to a certain extent, some teachers having been unwilling for students to read him. Some have seen him as patronising in the way he describes people and places, stressing the littleness of the city Tórshavn, wondering how one can have real houses and a real church in such a doll's house country. One wonders what complexes have caused such a reception. But there you have it, it's complicated.

During the 1960s a liberating change took place in Faroese poetry. Rhyme and regular rhythm was abandoned and along with the formal innovation came change on the thematic level. Both older poets and a number of young debutants joined the new trend. We won't mention all of them, but select a few interesting names. One of them is **Guðrið Helmsdal** (b. 1941) whose book of poems Lýtt lot (Warm breeze) 1963 was the first collection of poetry by a woman and also the first completely conducted in free verse. **Rói Patursson** (b. 1947) brought the beat of the anti-authoritarian rebellion in 1968 into the Faroese poetry world in a collection with no name from 1969. Later he has developed into a more introvert philosophical poet interested in modernist and postmodern questions: language as sign and contents, freedom and the limits of a poet's possibilities. Unfortunately Rói has not published any poems since his collection Líkasum (Just as) from 1985 which brought him the Nordic Council Literary Prize. He is currently the headmaster of The Folk High school. Our most controversial writer is **Carl Johan Jensen** (b. 1957) had his debut in 1979 as a lyricist and he has published a number of collections of poetry, investigating language and psyche on a high intellectual level. His poetry is not easily accessible to say the least; sometimes he uses his knowledge of Old Norse to coin his own vocabulary. Now looking in the rear view mirror his whole production was a preparation for his tour de force Ó-søgur um djevulskap (Un-stories of devilry) in 2007. He works as a writer and critic, and claims that his book Ósøgur (Un-stories) is the best book written in the Faroes in the last hundred years.[7]

During the 1980s we had several new prose writers. The little village in their case has become a distant memory – they have lived their lives in Tórshavn. The meeting between Faroese and foreign becomes a recurring motif in stories about young people leaving for Denmark to get an education, reassessing their own home in the light of foreign experiences. **Hanus Kamban** (b. 1942) has written several collections of short stories. His style is traditional, intellectual – lots of literary references. Recently Hanus published a 3 volume literary autobiography on Janus Djurhuus whom we mentioned earlier. He is currently working on a biography on the other Djurhuus brother Hans Andreas. **Gunnar Hoydal** (b. 1941)has written both poetry and prose. His novels – one of them has been translated into English, Under Southern Stars – are to a great extent autobiographical. In Under Southern Stars the story shifts all the time between the Faroes and the country in South America where the author lived some time as a child with his family. Between the present and

---

7.   http://www.nordic-literature.org/2006/nordisk/artikler/148.htm

the childhood, he draws from his memory and from different historical periods both in the Faroes and in South America. The style is characterized by density, parallelism and close presence. The book is a very interesting modern piece of literature.

The literary scene is, and always has been, male dominated. However, in the 1980s we saw several female authors trying their wings – markedly different from their male colleagues both in style and subject matter. It is worth mentioning that the reception was also markedly different. Some of them – notably **Marianna D. Dahl** (b. 1947) and **Bergtóra Hanusardóttir** (b. 1941) had such a rough handling by male critics that one wonders if they – the men – feel threatened. As in other countries we have had discussions about feminine and masculine style, and if feminine themes are less important than male ones etc. **Oddvør Johansen** (b. 1941) introduces modern female viewpoints into Faroese literature in her novel *Lívsins summar* (Summer of Life) from 1982. It takes place in Tórshavn and in a village during the 1950s, which of course is when she was a child herself, and it explores the lives of women in different situations. It is a feminist approach, but she is no man hater and indeed has objected to being called a feminist. Oddvør has written two other novels.

To end this part I've chosen a few women writers who are active now. Admittedly they are not as loud and conspicuous in the picture as the men, but they have talent and work hard. **Rakel Helmsdal** (b. 1966) writes very imaginative stories, both for children and adults. Her book *Søgur úr Port Janua* (Stories from Port Janua) in 1996, takes place in an imaginary town, and in one of her other books, you can find a map of Port Janua. Strange things happen to her people, who are interesting and have interesting names. In one story a family has just moved into a house and after a while they find a window which is only on the outside not on the inside. It turns out that a woman lives in a secret place under the house – we get this woman's family story. Rakel is

227

The author Rakul Helmsdal (b. 1966).
(From www.rit.fo – Official authors' union website)

currently working on a Nordic project with two other artists for a very popular series of books about *Skrímslið* (The monster).

Sólrun Michelsen (b. 1948) is not one of the youngest writers, but she didn't start writing until she had worked for many years and her children had grown up and left home. She writes children's books, but lately she has ventured into short stories (Tema við slankum/ Theme with aberrations). She focuses on extremely difficult topics involving people in crisis, and her simple prose goes right to your heart.

Marjun Kjelnæs (b. 1974) has entered several literary competitions. She won a short story competition and was second in another. Her first volume is Ein farri av kolvetni (A little bit of petrol). The main characters are marked by the disruption between their locked social position and their intangible longing to go abroad.

In 2009, 234 books were published in Faroese – 135 original works and 99 translations comprising: 21 fiction (13 original and 8 translations), 69 non-fiction (61 original and 8 translations), 28 school books and 116 children's books (33 original and 83 translations). The total number of Faroese books since the first volume in 1822 is 5,491 books. You can't make a living as a writer in the Faroes, you write in your spare time and during vacations. Many authors publish their own books, some of which would not pass a critical editor at a commercial publishing house. Interest and need rather than profit keep the wheels moving, and the lack of proper marketing movements gives great variation in the books published.[8]

There are two big subsidised publishing houses, one producing children's books and books for the young, and one doing school books. The lack of Faroese material for the whole educational system is always critical – obviously it is a challenge to compete with glittering books and electronical sites published in big countries for millions of people. They work on providing as much teaching material as possible for the schools, focusing on what others won't do: Faroese language, Faroese history, Faroese geography etc; but in some cases the students in the higher grades use Danish books. In my school the students use Danish books in many subjects – Danish English books for instance, which I find disconcerting because I think it is important to view the world with your own eyes and your own angle. Some teachers use English books to teach English which makes more sense.

8.   http://www.flb.fo/

The cultural scene in the Faroes offers a variety of artistic achievement, most of which is executed by amateurs . That goes for literature, pictorial art, music, theatre and film – film being a brand new twig on the cultural tree, consisting of a mini film school in Tórshavn for youngsters. However, in most areas there are ongoing efforts to introduce more professionalism, and also in most areas there are conflicts between amateurs and professionals. The most recent example concerning the art scene is where some artists have left the national gallery in protest and have started their own gallery. Not necessarily a bad thing, for in its wake the conflict carries a lot of discussions and deliberations about art. **Vencil** – named after Hammershaimb who we mentioned earlier – is a new literary magazine dedicated to quality texts in Faroese, prose and poetry, written in Faroese and translations. Every issue so far has given room for beginners, and the editors Arnbjørn Dalsgarð and Oddfríður Marni Rasmussen spend time on giving advice to young aspiring writers.

We have a national art gallery, a national theatre (with no theatre building yet) and there is a symphony orchestra with members from all over the country which gets together a couple of times a year. Faroese art has gone through much of the same development as literature with national romantic paintings of nature with a view of a village via expressionism and impressionism to abstract painting and experimenting young artists. The national gallery in Tórshavn offers examples of the different genres.

There is Faroese radio (since 1956) and TV (since the 1980s), but Faroese television has very little Faroese, transmitting American movies with Danish subtitles or Danish entertainment with no subtitles. Admittedly there are children's programmes with Faroese speech, but too few – although authorities, teachers and everybody agrees that giving the children Faroese programmes is the most important task for the state-owned media. We have many bands playing all kinds of music, always trying to become famous outside the Faroes, sometimes using Danish competitions as a stepping stone. Many of these bands sing in English, but some have utilised the the market's interest in the exotic and in folklore, singing Faroese with inspiration from ballads. And we have excellent lyrics that are to be found on cds and not books.

The **Nordic House** in Tórshavn is a centre for Scandinavian culture in the Faroes and Faroese culture in Scandinavia, inviting guests and arranging exhibitions and concerts both ways.

We are not an isolated group of islands any more, the way we were when Graba, Stanley and others came to watch the noble savages in their habitat. We communicate with the world, receiving impulses from all over the world. Our young people travel and bring back inspiration – well if they come back. Unfortunately many move away never to return … but that is another story.

Useful sites

http://www.heinesen.fo/faroeislandsreview/Articles.htm
    Articles, pictures, videos about the Faroes (in English)

http://www.flb.fo
    Library of the Faroes

http://www.sr.fo
    Faroese dancing and ballads, contains videos of the ring dance

http://art.fo/fo/
    The Faroese national gallery – has an English version of the site

http://www.haskulin.fo/Default.aspx?pageid=2249
    The history of the Folk High School in English

http://www.nlh.fo/Default.aspx?SectionId=214
    The Nordic house

http://www.setur.fo/en/university/
The Faroese University

http://www.rit.fo/default.asp?home=true
The Faroese writers' association

http://www.rakelhelmsdal.info/2008/byurin/byurin_intro.html
Rakel Helmsdal's homepage

http://www.framtak.com/info/faroese
The Faroese alphabet and numbers

Bibliography

Many foreign travellers to the Faroes have written diaries in which they describe the islands and the inhabitants:

Carl Julian Graba, *Dagbók skrivað á eini ferð til Føroya í árinum 1828,* (Bókagarður, 1987). Diary from 1828. Graba was German.

Jean Babtiste Charcot, *Ferðir til Føroya,* (Sprotin, 1994). Diary from 1901. Charcot was French.

The Journals of the Stanley Expedition to the Faroe Islands and Iceland in 1789, (Føroya Fróðskaparfelag, 1970). Stanley was British.

Kenneth Williamson, *The Atlantic Islands; a study of the Faroe life and scene* (1948).

G.C.V. Young, *From the Vikings to the Reformation: Chronicle of the Faroe Islands to 1538.*

Jens Christian Svabo, *Indberetninger fra en rejse udi Færø 1781–1782.*

Lucas Debes, *Færoæ & Færoa reserata 1673.*

Jørgen Landt, *Forsøg til en beskrivelse af Færøerne 1800.*

Islands Book Trust Commemorations to Mark the 80th Anniversary of the Evacuation of St Kilda

Limited edition envelopes and headed notepaper were available to those attending the St Kilda conference. They show eight scenes from St Kilda. The beautiful artwork for them was by artist Maureen Kerr who was employed as one of the chefs on the military base on the islands for ten years and gave up her job there in November 2010. Maureen used to live at Howmore on South Uist and has now moved to the island of Lismore near Oban. Covers purchased at the conference could be addressed and stamped with the specially designed St Kilda *smiler* postage stamp, then taken to St Kilda for posting. There the St Kilda World Heritage Site circular hand stamp was also applied in the St Kilda shop. The mail was then taken to Balivanich on Benbecula to be further stamped and posted at the local post office on Saturday 28th August 2010, the operational day closest to the anniversary (29th August 1930) of the evacuation. The post office in Balivanich (then known as Nunton post office) at one time held the St Kilda circular date stamp for outgoing mail from St Kilda en route to the mainland. This was withdrawn on the introduction of the Balivanich postmark.

Also, Neil Ferguson, grandson and namesake of the celebrated last St Kilda postmaster, launched a St Kilda mail boat off the island on Saturday 14th August 2010. Neil, who lives in

Maidens, Ayrshire, was one of a group of twenty-two who visited St Kilda after the conference. The mail boat was designed to hold some of the specially produced postal covers and a number of postcards. The mail boat was constructed by well-known Benbecula carpenter Donald MacDonald of Hacklet. Therein lies another connection with St Kilda – Donald's grandfather, Donald (Domhnall na Banaich), a well-known carpenter in his time, was involved in building work on the St Kilda church and manse. The mail boat was found on the west side of Lewis on Saturday 9th October 2010 by Mitchell Thompson, age thirteen, of 10 Brue.

Using proceeds from the special postal cover issue the Islands Book Trust has funded the restoration of two gravestones commemorating the lives of five St Kildans in Tulliallan cemetery in Kincardine-on-Forth. The gravestones have been polished and the lettering on them restored. The first of the two gravestones commemorates Finlay MacQueen (1862–1941), his daughter Mary Ann (1892–1970), and her husband, Neil Ferguson Jnr. (1899–1975). The second gravestone commemorates Neil Junior's parents, Ann MacQueen (1877–1940), and Neil Ferguson Senior (1876–1944). Photographs of the two gravestones, before and after restoration, were shown to members of the St Kilda Club at their annual reunion in Edinburgh on Saturday 20th November by Alasdair MacEachen from Benbecula, a trustee of the Islands Book Trust.

Last, but not least, Mrs Nancy MacDonald, widow of Lachie MacDonald, was presented at the conference with a certificate making her an honorary member of the Islands Book Trust. This was in recognition of her late husband's significant contribution to the collection of recordings and photographs, not only of life on St Kilda prior to the evacuation, but also through keeping up the St Kilda contacts after they moved off the island in 1930. The recordings include material provided for the School of Scottish Studies, Edinburgh University, the BBC and the National Trust of Scotland. Nancy visited St Kilda with Lachie in 1980 to commemorate the 50th anniversary of the evacuation and she still keeps in touch with many descendants now living throughout Scotland.